ACTIVATE THE BRAIN ~ STIMULATE YOUR BRAND!

KEN BANKS | ROBYN WINTERS

Edited by Denise McCabe/www.mccabeediting.com

ISBN: 1456427970
ISBN-13: 9781456427979
LCCN: 2010918154

Published by: BrainBranding LLC

Acknowledgments

From Ken Banks

Books like this do not result solely from a current research project or collaboration, but rather are the result of bringing into play the perspective and expertise that one gains from many years in a career that relates to the topic at hand. This is particularly true for me as I consider whom to acknowledge for the help and inspiration that made this book possible.

Certainly, the first person to recognize is my co-author, Robyn Winters, who inspired the whole idea of BrainBranding, based on our meeting at the National Speakers Association Annual Convention in 2007. We discovered that, while we came from completely different disciplines, we were in sync about how the concept of thinking styles and the principles of an effective brand strategy could work together to help companies and individuals create more successful brands. Robyn's creative thinking and attention to detail, as well as being an excellent taskmaster, were instrumental in making this book a reality.

Thanks also to the great marketers that I have worked with during my career at companies such as Eckerd, Doner, PetSmart, and Publicis, places where I was able to hone my skills and gain opportunities to try out exciting ways to make the brands I was responsible for come alive. My appreciation also to my colleagues at the Retail Advertising and Marketing Association, the National Retail Federation, Texas A&M, and the University of Florida for inspiration and education that have provided a perspective that has been invaluable to me over the years, and that contributed to the concepts described in this book.

Thanks especially to my wife Sandi, and my daughters Michelle and Lisa, for putting up with my absenteeism too often in a career filled with meetings, conventions, conferences, and other business trips that kept me on a plane more often than I would have liked. Their understanding and motivation through the years has been invaluable, and I love them for it.

Thanks to the National Speakers Association for its inspiration, and for the network of friends (especially my mastermind group) who have inspired me and provided candid feedback that has been so helpful along the way.

A successful brand is the result of building a relationship with your customers. The relationships I have had the honor to build throughout the years have been the key to the success I have achieved and the insights that are contained in this book.

From Robyn Winters

My passion for the psychology of human behavior and the understanding of people's natural thinking styles moved me to write this book with Ken Banks - my business partner, co-author, and friend. Working together, we took our two areas of expertise, combined and shaped them into a meaningful whole to share with readers we knew would benefit from our message. Ken's extensive background in marketing and retail provided the important foundation to make our concept both realistic and beneficial.

Ken and I met through the National Speakers Association. Over the past twenty years, NSA has provided me with a wealth of knowledge, insights. and connections, both to and through the speaking industry. I am forever indebted to this wonderful organization.

My small, mighty MasterMind group has provided continuous support and feedback during the writing process. Shari Bowden, our resident genius, physicist and author, provided viewpoints and perspectives that challenged me and kept me focused. Denise McCabe, my editor-at-large (and small), brought this book to life. I describe her as someone who smoothes out the bumps on the uneven path of writing. Denise's patience and expertise are nothing short of remarkable - she treats every written word she edits with tender loving care.

I'd also like to thank my dear friend Nancy Vann, whose spiritual guidance and uncompromising honesty (couldn't she fib just a little?) continues to keep me true and authentic - every day.

Another wonderful friend, Judith Ross, has been a stanchion of unconditional support and caring for more years than I will mention. As the Beatles once said, "I get by with a little help from my friends."

Finally, I would be remiss if I did not mention Jack Bloom, a wise and caring counselor from many years ago, who helped me to peel back the layers that uncovered who I was and who I could be, and started me on a path of self-discovery that continues to this day. It all began with you, Jack.

I am also grateful that Ken and I were able to share an "office away from the office," generously provided by the staff of two hotels: Justin Grogan, Angel Martinez, Colleen Predmore, Jamee Johnson, and Annette Dempsey from the Wyndham Tampa Westshore, and Tammy Straw from the InterContinental Hotel in Tampa.

We write acknowledgments because they underscore the value and necessity of positive, long-lasting, enduring relationships. To me, that's what BrainBranding is all about.

Table of Contents

foreword

Innovative approaches to selling products and services are the heartbeat of any business venture. In today's vernacular, the term to differentiate your products and services from those of other people is known as Branding.

Branding is the aspect of marketing that focuses on influencing prospects to believe that your products and services are the only ones that provide a solution to their problems. The impetus for this book, which takes a revolutionary and unique branding approach, stems from the combined efforts of Ken Banks and Robyn Winters to artfully merge the concept of branding with the brain's four Buying Styles. Together, they culminate in an original branding approach known as BrainBranding.

Many theorists have formed hypotheses on customer retention, buyer decision making, ways to market a new product or service, and the character of the sales process. But only BrainBranding expertly considers brand qualities *and* the buyer's style of thinking - into a well-thought-out process that assures success.

The authors synthesized their two areas of expertise into a strategy that enhances any company's positioning in the marketplace, ensuring that a brand stands out from its competition. BrainBranding proves to be an invaluable tool for *any* type of business that wants to establish a brand that resonates with everyone in its target market - and beyond.

The authors provide a coherent, well-defined BrainBranding model, essential to broadening consumer base and appeal. More than 25 existing business examples demonstrate how companies develop their brand strategy; but these same companies do not necessarily take into account how people draw on their Buying Styles to decide which brand to select. Had they used the BrainBranding approach, they could have capitalized on the fact that consumers' use of buying styles - based on their brains' thought processes - results in reasonably consistent purchasing decisions.

Banks and Winters drive home the fact that, among clients and prospects, there will be representatives of each of the four different buying styles. Therefore, learning about these buying styles and addressing them during the branding process can increase prospect interest and expand a potential client base.

Forms to develop a brand, using the BrainBranding process, are included to further facilitate individual or company branding efforts. In addition, the authors provide two start-to-finish case studies illustrating how this process works.

BrainBranding - the book - provides comprehensive techniques that broaden any company's or individual's brand appeal and improve their bottom line. In the final analysis, isn't that the primary goal of branding?

Authors Banks and Winters offer a distinctive and original system in BrainBranding. You won't be disappointed, I promise!

F. Felicia Ferrara, Ph.D.
Psychologist, Researcher, Speaker/Consultant

INTRODUCTION -

IS YOUR BRAND ALWAYS ON MY MIND?

Oprah. Donald Trump. Martha Stewart. Joyce. Joyce?

A few years ago, a major retailer conducted a meeting with a group of analysts to share their plans and strategies for growing market share over the next 12 months. While they had been relatively successful for the past several years, they were currently experiencing stagnation in sales and growth in market share. The company's CEO was enthusiastically explaining that they had defined their "target customer" more specifically than ever before in their history.

The CEO went on to say that, as a result of extensive research, the company had defined their ideal target customer so clearly, and with such detail, that they were able to personify her and give her a name - Joyce.

Who was Joyce? Among other items of demographic information, she was a 37-year-old working mother with two children and had a promising career and a strong commitment to her family and community. She and her husband enjoyed travel, cooking, and the arts. Joyce exercised regularly and loved photography and music.

There were many more details that helped the meeting attendees come to know her, and there was even a photo of Joyce and her family to help everyone recognize her more clearly! This description was followed by a discussion of her purchasing behavior, her likes and dislikes, and her tastes in clothing and home furnishings. Yes, they knew Joyce well and they fully expected her - and many like her - to spend a lot of time and money in their redesigned stores.

Eighteen months later, the CEO was gone and so was Joyce - casualties of an ongoing slump in sales and a loss in market share to the store's major competitors.

What Went Wrong?

There were several reasons attributed to the advertising campaign's lack of success, despite all of the research and the details amassed about their target. Was the brand strategy wrong? Was the economy keeping customers like Joyce away from their stores? Were the stores not operating with the consistency they expected?

It may have been some or all of these reasons. Or, it could be that the company and its management team had narrowed their focus so well that they were missing many of their potential customers: they had tried to communicate their brand so specifically to the Joyces of the world that their message was never heard by the several *other* types of customers who would shop in their stores. And perhaps Joyce needed more reasons to shop than their research uncovered.

We believe it's a matter of understanding not just who Joyce is but how Joyce thinks — how she and her counterparts make decisions about what to buy and where to buy it. Joyce shops at a store for many reasons, but she wants a relationship with the store. She

wants to know what it's famous for and why she should go there on a consistent basis.

This particular store was not the only one whose marketing decisions missed the goal. A few years ago, at the National Retail Federation's annual conference in New York City, we attended a panel discussion on the main stage by the CEOs of three of the top companies in the industry. All of them talked about the importance of building a relationship with their customers, and focusing their efforts on building a brand that maintained a loyal customer base. Efficiency, they believed, would come from specifically tailoring the company's message, and that this would lead to success.

We couldn't help but believe that Joyce had long since left the room - just like the CEO who had extolled the virtues of targeting so specifically. We were also convinced that brand success depends not only on building customer relationships, but also on appealing to *all* the motivators that define an individual's buying habits - not just one or two.

A New Partnership is Formed

A couple of months after the New York conference, we met up at the National Speakers Association convention and, after a lengthy discussion, recognized the synergy between branding and thinking/ buying styles. We realized that, in order for businesses or individuals to be truly successfully, they need to include the dynamics of thinking style with their branding strategy.

As we continued to explore the idea of blending innovative branding strategies with Buying Styles, we could envision the tremendous potential in combining these two elements to create brands that

would resonate more completely and effectively within targeted markets - or any markets. This is particularly important when you realize that people are composites, and more than one style is usually responsible for the decisions people make regarding the products and services they buy. Which is precisely why the profile of Joyce was unsuccessful: the narrower the focus, the fewer parts of the brain that are engaged, and the fewer people who are drawn to your brand.

Our discussions continued. We gave presentations to an array of organizations, companies, and individuals. The more we shared between ourselves and with other professionals, the more we realized there was an invaluable message for anyone looking to strengthen their brand.

The result of our experiences formed the foundation of this book. Its purpose is to help you appreciate, more clearly and concisely, why branding is so critical to achieving success in business. In the process, we also provide an in-depth discussion about your brain and the factors that contribute to the purchasing process: why some people react one way to brands and marketing messages, while others don't react at all. It's part art, part science, and a lot of common sense.

While we recognize that there is a great deal of literature and discussion about branding, there is also an equal amount of misconception about what a brand truly is, and how important a BrainBrand is to your success.

What's In It For You?

By applying the principles, logic and your own BrainBranding worksheets in this book, you'll have the tools to determine your true brand and brand value. Understanding branding is not unlike knowing your own DNA: developing a more effective brand will result in a deeper knowledge of what your brand is, and create an enduring brand persona built to foster meaningful, long-term relationships.

The examples we use represent the brands of many different companies and individuals - some successful and some that have floundered. However, they will serve as benchmarks for the premise behind BrainBranding.

It's the understanding of this principle that drives the BrainBranding process; it's also dictated the way we chose to present our material and insights to you. As a result, you will develop a level of branding expertise that will accelerate your success and assure your own personal satisfaction.

Our Target Readers

This book will have particular value to the following groups:

- Marketing Professionals
- Entrepreneurs
- Speakers/Presenters
- Consultants
- Internal Employees
- Aspiring Managers

When you develop a successful brand for your business, you are simultaneously developing a personal brand for yourself. This will go a long way to help you with your career - either within a company, in your own business, or in planning your future. The principles are

the same and the steps are applicable - no matter what the branding challenge.

So whether you're an aspiring marketing staff member at a major packaged goods or service organization, or embarking on a second, third, or new career, you'll find that these tenets can be applied anytime there is a need for differentiating your unique value.

It's time to unleash the power of the brain and apply it to your brand. BrainBranding is not just a solution - it's a process to determine what you can do to be even more successful. Apply the principles. Personalize them to your own situation. Watch the results.

Note: At the end of Chapters 4-7, there will be a section titled "Developing Your Brand," where you will have the opportunity to build your brand and to individualize your own BrainBranding process.

CHAPTER 1:

DIFFERENTIATION - DEFINE YOUR BRAND

Recently, we submitted a proposal to a major conference to present our BrainBranding workshop. We described our presentation as a revolutionary way to look at branding that would inspire audience members to enhance their company's brands and increase brand appeal to their clients and customers. It was a thorough proposal that we felt clearly defined our branding approach and its benefits.

Shortly after we submitted it, we received a call from the meeting planner, who was in the midst of selecting speakers from among a number of proposals. We were having a good conversation, going into even more depth about our concept: how it would be an innovative approach that attendees would not have heard before, and one they would be able to apply to their business when they returned to work.

We were pumped up by the conversation until the planner asked this question: "Don't you think that branding is an overused topic that doesn't generate much interest to our audience?" "Overused"? "Doesn't generate much interest??" To us that would be like saying that audiences aren't interested in presentations to "improve

> *Lexus marketed itself to appeal to the four "buying styles," stressing four distinct qualities in their marketing efforts.*

profits" or "generate sales" or "gain more clients." These topics never get old to people who want a successful business, and we don't believe that "branding" will ever be out of date either. And that's what she came to understand.

Lexus - "The Pursuit of Perfection"

A Successfully Defined Brand Appeals to All Four Buying Styles

Let's consider the case of one of the most successful brand introductions in the past several years - Lexus. Toyota introduced its first entry into the luxury car market the same year that Nissan introduced its Infiniti model - in the identical category and to the identical group of target customers.

The cars were basically the same, from features to performance to pricing. However, the disparity in the sales of these brands for the first several years was as different as a Chevy Aveo is from a Mercedes SL550. Lexus not only became the number one choice among luxury cars in the United States, but also the standard of comparison for luxury automobiles - then, and for years to come.

Why? Because of *branding*. Lexus marketed itself to appeal to the four "buying styles" of the brain by stressing four distinct qualities in their marketing efforts:

1. Styling and features that made it the choice of discriminating car buyers

2. The best service record in the industry, which appealed to those looking for dependability
3. Superior ratings from Lexus customers in national polls
4. Innovative technology and mechanical features that have set the standard for those who are looking for the cutting edge extras that define a luxury automobile

Simultaneously, while Infiniti was recognized for strong performance and a nimble drive, its marketing focused more on the esoteric experience one might get from driving their cars. In their advertising campaign, the viewer would see lovely views of the car winding its way through country roads while leaves floated through the air. Customers had a difficult time discerning which features made it distinctive among similar cars in its class.

In other words, Lexus *branded* its new car, while Infiniti simply advertised a feeling. Branding for Lexus meant creating the very essence of the car, an essence that would resonate with prospective customers and immediately define its unique value to them.

So why then would someone wonder if branding is old news? It could very well be that many people - including those in the marketing business - have the wrong idea about the true meaning of branding. They think of branding as logos, slogans, new ad campaigns, new names, packaging, and signage. Yes, these are all methods to communicate a brand, but they are not the brand itself.

Just as your own unique DNA distinguishes who you are, the brand is the core of why a product, service, or store was created, and why it should be the preferred choice by its targeted customers.

What is a Brand?

We believe that Dr. Leonard Berry, founder of the Center for Retail Studies at Texas A&M University, and one of today's top scholars in customer service and marketing, said it best:

> **"A brand is not only what the *company says* it is, but also what the *customer thinks* it is. Companies with the strongest brands stand for something that is important to targeted customers. They have answered the question: 'What do we want to be *famous for* with our customers?'"**

Branding is not simply awareness. You may have seen a sign or an ad for a product several times, but have no feeling about it or understanding of what it does. If you have no relationship with the product, store, or service, then there is no brand. Period.

The brand is the DNA of your business, and it represents everything that differentiates it from the other similar brands on the market. Just as your own unique DNA distinguishes who you are, the brand is the core of why a product, store, or service was created, and why it should be the preferred choice by its targeted customers.

Is this a new concept? Of course not. For hundreds of years, successful brands have defined and redefined who they are in the quest for more sales and market share. As Peter Montoya says, "A brand is *an identity that stimulates a precise and meaningful perception about what you stand for.*" Here's a well-known example.

Kmart - "Right Here. Right Now."

Kmart Misses the Point

There's a reason why this brand was by far the number one choice in the discount store category for many years, and was then left trailing in the dust by Walmart. And it had nothing to do with price. Both companies had - and still have - a strong, low price perception. However, Walmart lives up to its brand every day by ensuring that it will have what the customer wants: in-stock items, at a low price, in well-kept stores that are serviced by associates who truly care. And those qualities are the qualities that separate one brand from another. Let's examine the "rebranding" of Kmart.

Less than a decade ago, as Walmart aggressively took market share away from the former discount king, Kmart decided to *rebrand* itself as "Big Kmart." We have done a great deal of research that indicates Kmart was one of the top retail choices. The fact that it was "small" never came up as a weakness that would steer shoppers to another store. Never.

Kmart must have thought that size was a differentiator, because they launched a multimillion-dollar ad campaign to introduce the new Big Kmart.

The Big K/Kmart Story

A fresh campaign featuring Bob Hope (just before he died) was supported with an aggressive print campaign, new signs on most stores, new badges, new paint inside and out, and some new product offerings. Otherwise, it was business as usual.

What's It All About?

When customers wanted to find out what the new "Big-ness" was all about, they were in for a surprise. For example, we went into a local Big Kmart and stopped by the sporting goods department, which had been one of Kmart's differentiating categories for years. There was an associate, Myrt, who was at least 70 years old and had been with the store...well, forever. And it's doubtful that she had ever fished in her life much less played soccer, baseball, golf, or tennis for that matter.

But there she was, "managing" the department, along with Ev, who could have been Myrt's older sister and who was stocking some of the shelves. When asked what they thought of their store's new branding, they looked at each other and Myrt said, "Hmmm, I don't see much difference. Oh, we got new badges. And the sign out front is new. Otherwise, it's same old, same old."

So typical, to spend millions of dollars on a campaign that doesn't seem to have any distinctive messages, and then fail to even clue in the employees about why you're doing it. Is there any wonder that, after all the mergers, store closings and consolidation with Sears (another brand in need) that, on any given day, you can walk into Kmart and see one register checkout manned with a real person and one or two customers. While right down the road, Walmart is buzzing with activity at 6-10 registers, with several customers at each one.

> *Once you understand what branding is all about, you can begin to define your differentiating factors in an effective way - to your clients and customers, and to your associates.*

Hummer - "Like Nothing Else"

GM's Shining Star

Hummer is another example of the value of branding. When GM introduced the Hummer to the consumer market in 1991, they built on its brand reputation as a military transport vehicle: tough, durable vehicles that appeal to a public that already says it prefers SUVs and pickups more than conventional sedans and coupes. Its designs and looks were featured in displays that simulated rock climbing in front of the dealerships and its interiors were rugged yet stylish.

In a way, they were similar to Rolex watches: chunky, but easily identifiable as something more expensive and definitely reflective of a successful lifestyle. The brand fostered a number of other products and games that furthered its macho image, and was one of the great success stories at GM, while its other brands suffered.

Today, even with a downturn in the economy, the Hummer still maintains a consistent, positive image with its customers and has the potential to reenergize its customer base in the future.

While many people recognize the importance of branding, they shortchange their branding efforts by thinking of them solely as a function of marketing. Case in point: how we teach branding to our future marketers.

Branding or Marketing - Get Your Priorities Straight

At many universities around the country with graduate-level marketing courses, the textbook that is used is *Essentials of*

> *Until we define what the brand is in real business terms... it will continue to remain a sluggish performer...*

Marketing by William Perreault, Jr., Joseph Cannon and E. Jerome McCarthy. This is a terrific textbook that is well written, with many solid examples to make the information more applicable and memorable. It even includes a CD with additional videos and examples, to make the learning more interesting and effective.

What is amazing is that, out of the 646 pages of sound marketing content, there are only *seven pages* devoted to branding. These pages talk about executable activities such as logos, packaging, and slogans, yet fail to emphasize the importance of branding to the total business proposition.

We tend to leave branding to the marketing department. If, in fact, it really is the DNA of the product/service/store, it should be a focus of the entire organization, from the CEO to the sales associate and shipping room personnel. Until we define what the brand is in real business terms, and not just in marketing executions, the brand will continue to remain a sluggish performer with little or no consumer loyalty.

But wait - there is hope! The BrainBranding process puts your brand back in the spotlight where it belongs, and creates a distinct and unique DNA for your product or service. It is, in fact, the solution.

CHAPTER 2:

WHAT YOU BUY, AND WHY YOU BUY IT

If you were to line up different types of objects, such as cars, houses, or coffee cups, and then if you were to consider the pros and cons of which ones to buy, those decisions would be governed by your mental processes - how you think.

Since 450 B.C., when Hippocrates identified four temperaments, psychologists, psychiatrists, scientists, and researchers have analyzed not only temperaments, but also personality types, behaviors, and thinking styles - all with different perspectives, yet with a similar conclusion:

> As human beings, your behaviors and personalities, your preferences and proclivities, strongly influence what you do and why you do it.

A number of models demonstrating predicted behavior continue to find popularity today, both in and out of the workplace. Below are examples of well-known model-based assessments. We have developed a behavioral model as well, which is described later in this chapter.

Assessment/Model Examples

- **The Myers-Briggs Type Indicator (MBTI) - Personality**
  This scientifically-validated assessment is designed to measure *psychological* preferences in the ways people perceive the world and make decisions. The original developers of the personality inventory were the team of Katharine Cook Briggs and her daughter, Isabel Briggs Myers, who based the assessment on the research of Swiss psychologist Carl Jung.

  The MBTI identifies 16 personality types that result from the combinations of **four preference scales**: (1) Extroversion / Introversion, (2) Sensing / Intuition, (3) Thinking / Feeling, and (4) Judging / Perceiving.

- **The DISC Model - Behavior**
  The DISC is a validated, non-scientific system, and the model is based on the work of behaviorist William Moulton Marston. It examines the behavior of individuals in their environment, or within a specific situation in that environment.

  DISC is an acronym for these four aspects of behavior: **D**ominance - relating to control, power and assertiveness; **I**nfluence - relating to social situations and communication; **S**teadiness - relating to patience, persistence, and thoughtfulness; and **C**onscientiousness - relating to structure and organization.

- **Emergenetics - Brain-Based**
  Emergenetics is a brain-based psychometric assessment that highlights thinking and behavior. Its purpose is to provide a means to gain a clearer understanding of how people live, work,

communicate, and interact. It is built on four thinking and three behavioral attributes that are measured independently.

Other assessments, such as Tracom's Social Style decision-making model, and the CORE Profile Paradigm personality assessment, are widely used today by an array of companies for professional development and hiring purposes. In addition, individuals and teams take advantage of these models to enhance to enhance personal growth and development.

What these different models share in common is that they've identified four distinct approaches to each of their premises, whether it's thinking style, personality, or behavior-based.

The Bottom Line

The models described above also demonstrate how the brain, or mind, or mental processes influence what you do, how and why you do it, and how you feel about the what, why, and how of what you do.

The fact is that everyone's brains are different, which explains why people are attracted to particular - and different - brands and what the brands have to offer. There are, in fact, definite "triggers" that the brain responds to that provide the impulse to select one brand over another - not just once, but time after time.

Consider this: most people don't think before they write - they just write. If you were to pick up a pen to write your name, would you think, "Which hand should I use - right or left?" Probably not, because the choice will be instinctive. Making buying decisions becomes instinctive as well. Just look in your closet at the clothes you've bought over the years and you'll see what we mean.

It's extremely important to create a brand that capitalizes on the ways people think and make buying decisions, because your brand and marketing strategy will be more successful when it engages the brain, mind, and hearts of *all* buying styles, thinking and behavioral styles, and personality types. You will greatly increase your market share, because your brand will have more universal appeal. This is not just branding - it's BrainBranding.

How Your Brain Looks at a Brand

Based on the research of industrial psychologist Carl Rogers, we know that the average person speaks at a rate of about 200-250 words per minute. The average person also processes what is being said at approximately 600-800 words per minute. What does your brain do with the lag time? It moves on to something else!

The brain figures things out in blur-like speed, continuously making often-unconscious decisions about what it will and will not pay attention to. Here's an example. You may have experienced a scenario where someone is speaking to you, and you're listening carefully at the beginning of the discussion. But then your brain starts to assume what the other person is going to say next (because it's far ahead), or is not engaged because of the words being used, so it moves on. In fact, to the other person, it may even appear that you're still listening intently. Sound familiar?

What Your Brain Looks for in a Brand

Your brain is a selective filter - for listening, working, communicating, and all its everyday processing needs. The same holds true when it makes a decision about brands. Some things are filtered in, and others are filtered out. The above diagram illustrates the four possibilities that your brain is seeking in a brand:

When you are deciding on a brand, your brain has certain preferences that it looks for - preferences that match its buying style. It looks for answers to some or all of the following questions:

1. Authentication (about the product or service):

- How long has the company or brand been doing business?
- What has been written about it?

- What do the sales figures indicate?
- Who has endorsed it, and has that endorsement been substantiated?
- What are the credentials of those in charge?

The following is an example of a brain that seeks Authentication.

Morgan Stanley/Smith Barney - "We Make Money the Old Fashioned Way. We Earn It."

Before it merged with Morgan Stanley, Smith Barney had long established itself as one of the blue-blood stock brokerages on Wall Street. The firm had developed its brand over a period of many years, with a solid record of accomplishment of providing its clients with consistently solid returns on their portfolios. Their reputation was based not on flashy performance or marketing, but rather on a reputation of working hard to provide clients with the best information and insights that were based on solid research and in-depth analysis by its staff of experts.

When the need arose to become more public with its marketing in order to continually grow its revenues, Smith Barney conducted research on why so many of their clients had been loyal over many years - or even for generations. It discovered that these clients truly believed that the firm worked harder than other brokerage to maximize their returns. The resulting campaign, which won many awards, was extremely successful in positioning Smith Barney as the firm that "made money the old-fashioned way...they earned it."

Clients who were more fact-based looked for Authentication, founded on a solid history of long-term performance, chose Smith Barney and maintained their loyalty over time.

2. Organization (the structure of brand and marketing information):

- What's the history of this company or brand?
- How is it regulated?
- What are the associated risk factors?
- Do they have a well-thought-out business and marketing plan that makes sense? Is there consistency between the brand, its practices, and its procedures?
- Is the marketing message consistent with the brand?

The following is an example of how the brain looks for Organization.

IBM - "Solutions for a Small Planet"

IBM has been one of the most powerful companies in providing corporations and individuals with a solid line of business equipment - even before computers took over the world.

IBM built its brand not only on the constant innovation of new machines and technology to help in the corporate marketplace, but also on how they differentiated themselves, based on the quality of the people who made up a deep, well-educated, highly specialized organization.

Customers wanted the technology generated by mainframes as well as PCs and printers; what the customers also wanted was the expertise that IBM provided, which included the precise equipment to meet their needs, and the ability to work with them in developing their plans with a structure that would equip them for any contingencies.

3. Connection (how you're captured emotionally by a person, product or service).

- How do you feel doing business with this brand, product or service?
- How will it benefit you, your business, or your family?
- Will you be able to form a relationship that is sustainable over time?
- Are you more than just a sale to them?
- Will there a consistent person who will stay in touch?

The following is an example of how the brain seeks out Connection.

Hallmark - "When You Care Enough to Send the Very Best"

One of the greatest ways that individuals maintain contact with family, friends, customers, and clients is through the use of greeting cards. It's no secret that Hallmark lives up to its name as the standard for providing the best selection of cards with just the right messages for its customers. The company has been successful at fulfilling this mission for over a century, and its brand has been based on the connection that they have worked hard to maintain with those who rely on Hallmark to find just the right sentiments - day after day, year after year.

Hallmark's branding has been consistent for these 100 years with messages as poignant and as well targeted as those in the cards they sell. In creating its own programming (the Hallmark Hall of Fame series of outstanding movies) and then its own network (the Hallmark Channel), they have provided a medium for their message that is consistent in bringing emotions and warm feelings to

TV screens in millions of homes - much in the same way that it has been relaying these same feelings through greeting cards for decades.

Uniform in quality, wholesomeness, and creativity, the Hallmark brand has differentiated itself in peak card-giving seasons with programs and messages that have made its customers and the recipients of their cards look on the back of the card for the Hallmark logo as reassurance of the sincerity of the message and its connection to the sender.

4. Imagination (how you visualize yourself and your business using the brand's products or services):

- Why is this brand, product, or service the right one for me?
- How will it positively change the way I do business or my way of life?
- What makes it distinctive?
- What are the possibilities if we work together?
- How will things change in 1 year? 5 years?

The following is an example of how the brain explores Imagination.

AT&T - "Rethink Possible"

The competition in the wireless communications industry has been as strong as any industry in consumer marketing over the past few years. AT&T Wireless has long built its brand on the history of the original telephone company that dominated the scene for decades. In the wireless business, it's been a different story, as AT&T has had to fight for market share as it continues to provide innovative programs and services.

With the intense competition, from Verizon and T-Mobile in particular, AT&T has built its brand differential on its connection speed as well as coverage. However, AT&T focuses its message on the customer's imagination of what might happen if a call doesn't get through just in time. From a near-miss meeting of a couple whose son eventually becomes president, to getting tickets to a football game that inspires a young boy to become a professional player, the marketing campaign stresses the personal importance of being on the cutting edge - without over-emphasizing the technology behind the fast speed of connections that AT&T provides.

Since we know that brands and brand characteristics create impulses in the brain, and that there are four different categories of impulses, you and your brand need to continually incorporate the qualities and characteristics that attract each of the four buying styles - every time.

Said another way, rather than narrow your focus to people you perceive to be in your target market, you need to *broaden* it to include the brain's four buying styles.

An Introduction to Buying Styles

This is a good time to formally introduce you to the four Buying Styles. As you read the descriptions, consider which one(s) mirror your instinctive purchasing preferences, and how they might influence the way you market your own brand.

The buying styles listed below will help you begin to identify who you are - and to characterize the DNA of your brand.

The Four Buying Styles

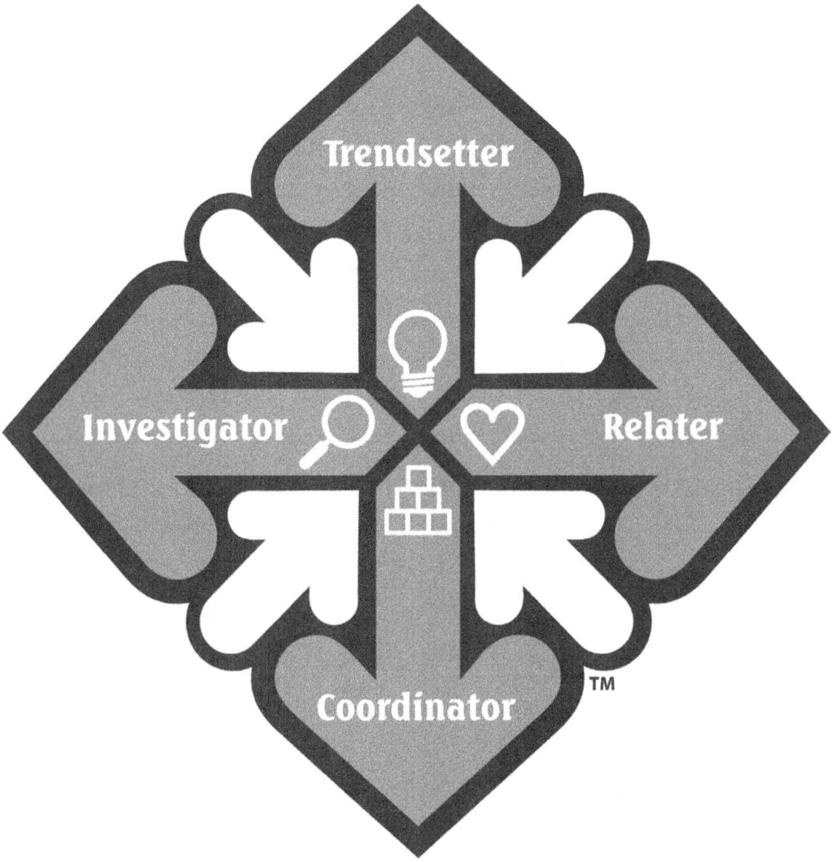

Following is a detailed description of each of the brain's four buying styles. You might want to check the key characteristics that most resonate with you.

The Investigator

The **Investigator** Style is diligent in conducting research prior to selecting a brand or making a purchase. It examines statistics, data, and information - not just about the item to be purchased, but that of competitive products or services. This style is likely to conduct a cost/benefit analysis, taking into account price versus resale value. The **Investigator** uses the Internet as a research tool, taking advantage of search engine speed and efficiency to scan articles and data before coming to a logical buying decision.

The **Investigator** is analytical, objective, and quantitative, and not swayed by emotional elements (e.g., "it's attractive;" "the salesperson is very helpful"). Just the facts, no theory, conjecture or feelings, please. Once the facts have been weighed, the **Investigator** is ready to make a decision and quickly move on.

The **Investigator** is not necessarily loyal to a particular brand - price, easy availability, and Internet ordering are important qualities to this buyer.

Here is a net-net summary of this style's characteristics and preferences:

- Competitive pricing
- Internet ordering or self-service in store
- Cost/benefit comparison
- Bottom-line impact of products/services

- Limited brand loyalty
- Decisions based on facts
- Gathers information first
- Values technical information

Bottom Line: The Investigator is looking for Authentication.

Progressive Insurance - "Think Easier. Think Progressive."

Progressive Insurance knows that insurance prospects are seeking Authentication - a way to validate that they are making the right choice every time the renewal notice comes in the mail.

As one of the top three direct sellers of insurance (especially automotive policies), Progressive has developed a brand based on the promise of making it easier for its customers to find not only the best prices, but also to tailor the type of coverage to their specific needs and lifestyles.

To communicate with this **Investigator** prospect, the company built its branding around a campaign featuring a make-believe insurance shopping mart where the host helps each customer (and sometimes its competitors' employees) to find just the right policy for their requirements, while demonstrating a comparison of the Progressive premium with other companies the customers are considering. It even features an imaginary scanning gun to quickly get the features into the computer to come up with the right policy.

The message is very clear to the customer who goes online to check out all of the alternatives in selecting and saving on the right policy. Progressive presents the facts and rationale, and guides people to make the right choice.

The Coordinator

Before making a purchase, the **Coordinator** style develops a prioritized list: which brands or items to consider, the qualities that are most important, a survey of what other people have said about it, and whether it's a practical investment. If a major purchase is involved, such as a car or appliance, then maintenance history, safety, and durability become important factors.

In a retail establishment, the **Coordinator** prefers a clean, well-organized store layout, one that is easy to navigate, with ample signage to point the way. In particular, if this style visits a store that has multiple locations, it prefers that the same layout be duplicated in each location. (CVS does a great job at this!).

The **Coordinator** amasses a great deal of information prior to a purchase, and then organizes those details into a system that facilitates the decision-making process.

Here is a summary of this style's characteristics and preferences:

- Well-structured information
- Consistency among store layouts
- Details of maintenance history
- Reliable, dependable features

- Practicality of products/ services
- Solution over style
- Implementation and usage options
- Clearly defined features

Bottom Line: The Coordinator is looking for Organization.

Volvo - "For Life"

The Swedish automaker, Volvo, has built its reputation in the United States as the safest vehicles on the road. This reputation is based on its historical performance in crash tests, as well as on the road.

While becoming more stylish in order to maintain its competitive position, Volvo has stayed true to its Scandinavian roots by touting the detail and standards that the organization has built into each vehicle it sells.

One of Volvo's key marketing messages has been to establish procedures that enable buyers to purchase the car at the factory in Sweden and bring it back to the States. The program is set up so that the buyer not only saves money in making the trip, but also helps the customer to experience what the organization does to ensure the quality of every vehicle it builds and sells.

Volvo's messages promote the company's engineering technology, environmental awareness, and focus on quality as values that the **Coordinator** is looking for, while still looking for stylish design and driving fun. They know that their buyer is interested in the history of the company (it has its own museum) as well as what goes into the building of each car. Its website is more informative than that of any other car company, and its potential customers relate well to this organized approach.

The Relater

The **Relater** has a buying style that is focused on people and relationships. First and foremost, it wants to make a connection - with the person from whom the purchase will be made and, ultimately, with the brand. And **Relaters** prefer to maintain that relationship over time. They don't just make a purchase - they make a friend for life.

The **Relater** has a gut-level, emotional response to a product or service, and creates an emotional bond to a brand. Think about how you've responded to the look of a shiny new car, or a salesperson with a truly consultative approach - that's what makes this style responsive. For this buying style, the experience is at least as important as the purchase itself.

The **Relater** analyzes behavior, not numbers. How am I treated? How friendly are the people I'm dealing with? Are they putting my interests before their needs? How will this benefit me (and my business, colleagues, family)? The answers to these questions form the basis for buying decisions, and create extreme brand/person loyalty.

Here is the story about this style's characteristics and preferences:

- Friendliness of sales person/staff
- Personalized services
- Emotional connection to the brand
- After-sale follow-up

- Fierce brand loyalty once established
- Brands that are fun
- Well-defined benefits
- A positive purchase experience

Bottom Line: The Relater is looking for Connection.

Chico's - "Most Amazing Personal Service"

There are many brands to select from when it comes to women's fashion stores. When you walk through a typical major mall in any city, one store is often hard to distinguish from another. Chico's, on the other hand, goes far beyond effective window displays to become a destination store for many of today's professional women.

Chico's recognized this need for brand differentiation when they developed their brand for a more mature woman (meaning not teens or students) who might have a family, a job, and outside interests - and still want to keep up with the latest fashion trends.

Starting with merchandise that relates to this lifestyle, Chico's knew that their brand was going to depend as much on the people selling the clothes (and how they looked wearing the Chico's line) as on the merchandise on the racks and display counters.

The company hired sales people who could identify with their customers - and who the customers can identify with. They hired people who could relate to their customers, and who where as enthusiastic about Chico's "the company" as the customers were about Chico's clothes. Then they built a promotional program - Chico's Passport Club - to reward customers for their loyalty as well as for providing feedback on what they liked and wanted every time they shopped for clothes in the store.

In an era of self-service and relative indifference, Chico's has found that relationships really do build the brand.

The Trendsetter

The **Trendsetter** is characterized by innovation. What's new? What's in? Does this brand fit the vision I have for myself and my business? The **Trendsetter** is willing to take a chance on new and relatively untried products, and may not be swayed by what others think and say. For example, they would stand in line to get the first iPad, or test drive a new-model automobile.

Trendsetters seek out artistry and originality - in the world outside them and in their own environment. So as a consumer, the **Trendsetter** style looks for items that are unique, beautiful, and innovative. This style can visualize how a purchase will fulfill a dream or destiny, and anticipates being on the cutting edge.

Here is a picture of this style's characteristics and preferences:

- Visionary marketing strategies
- Time to make decisions
- Creative, cutting-edge design
- State-of-the art concepts
- Original products/ services
- Long-term brand application
- Multiple options for brand usage
- A conceptual framework

Bottom Line: The Trendsetter is looking for Imagination.

DROID by Motorola - "The Next Generation of Does"

It would be easy to reiterate our discussion about Apple and its stores when talking about a trendsetting brand, but let's examine Apple's latest competitor from Motorola. The iPhone has been a revolutionary success, and for a competitor to just come out and "me-too" itself as another smart phone system would not establish any brand loyalty.

Motorola broke the mold with its introduction of the Android operating system from Google. While the system is available in many brands of smart phones, Motorola introduced the Droid to the public with a branding campaign that combined a customer's natural curiosity with a desire to attract the trendsetter who wanted not just something new, but something that made a statement about the savviness of its buyers.

The results have been amazing - not only for Motorola in reviving its wireless brand - but also for all the other devices competing with the iPhone and IPads and their breakthrough positioning.

A Well-Rounded Brand

Most people make decisions based on the triggers from more than one of their possible four buying styles, making it difficult to predict how any individual, or market segment, will make purchasing selections. That's why it's important to develop a well-rounded brand, one that appeals to all four buying styles. Rather than narrow

your focus, you will want to make it more comprehensive, in order to include *all* buying styles.

L.L. Bean - "Guaranteed. You Have Our Word"

The wearers of the L.L. BEAN clothing line are examples of people whose style *is* their brand (i.e., a tailored, conservative look, yet down-to-earth). L.L. Bean is a retail brand that targets a unique lifestyle better than many, and it has been doing so for nearly a hundred years. Of course, there are more powerful brands and more recognizable labels, but L.L. Bean has defined a way of life that includes each of the four buying styles, in a way that appeals to an outdoors, traditional customer who might also be equipped with an IPad and who drives a Lexus.

Built on the tradition of being one of the first direct marketers - through its catalogs and later its website - L.L. Bean has built its brand on an understanding that there is something special about the outdoor life that includes - and almost requires - the fashion and functionality of its merchandise. It has built a brand that its customers can easily identify with in their own lives, with memories and experiences that, over the years, have made it special. Its products and its services are old-fashioned in feel but high tech in delivery. At the same time, it maintains a satisfaction guarantee that has become legendary.

Questions to Consider

Now that you have foundational information about thinking styles, and you have an idea about your own unique buying style, here are two questions for you to consider:

1. *What motivates you to select one brand over another?* Your instinctive approach to thinking determines your motivation in selecting a brand, product, or service. Once you understand your natural pull towards a brand, and the marketing around that brand, you can fill in the blanks.

   The next logical step is to ask yourself what elements might be missing from your own brand development, ones that don't include certain key ingredients from other buying styles.

2. *What criteria did you consider in a recent significant purchase (e.g., car, appliance, home)?* Here are some possibilities:

   - Price
   - Availability
   - Reliability
   - Emotional connection

   - Innovation
   - Maintenance
   - Personal touch
   - Style

Whichever ones you considered - and there are many - they will provide you with clues about your personal triggers, and the impact your own thinking and buying styles have on the way you currently brand yourself, your work, or your business.

The best branding solution is one in which you take into account all four buying styles in the brain - so that your brand is not filtered out!

Putting It All Together - Where You See Yourself

Now that you have a clearer picture of the four Buying Styles and some of the traits that identify each of them, where do you see yourself? This is an important question, because your style "colors" everything you do: it forms the basis for how you develop your brand, how you perceive other brands and, importantly, it determines where you place your buying power.

Remember: it is natural to develop a brand based on your own buying style(s), because that's what is foremost in your mind. However, you increase your brand's marketability when you take other buying styles into consideration when developing a brand strategy.

The Implications of Buying Styles

Looking back, you have probably identified several Buying Style characteristics - the area(s) of your brain that hold the primary "triggers" that are put into play when you select a brand, product, or service. You are drawn to a brand by features and benefits that appeal to your most dominant preferences - the ones that are most instinctive for you, and that most keenly and frequently define your purchasing behaviors.

However, as you become even more interested in a brand, your brain starts kicking into action and other preferences begin to weigh in on the decision. You may be attracted to a brand because of its style or design, but when you start to consider it more seriously, factors like price, quality, features, and reliability become important as the **Investigator Style** becomes a player.

Or, you may seek another person's opinion or help in making the selection, to reassure yourself that you are making the best decision. That's when the **Relater Style** in your head decides to chime in… and so on.

Based on the strength of your thinking preferences, and the order in which they "kick in," your buying decisions are layered. But make no mistake, the four voices in your head have opinions, some stronger than others, and that's how your buying decisions are ultimately made.

Staples - "That Was Easy"

A friend of ours told us recently about her experience in purchasing a new laptop from Staples, an experience that demonstrates how these triggers become activated as you go through the buying process.

Our friend readily admits that the first reference point for her new laptop was color - she wanted a RED one. No other technical factors entered her mind as she began the initial online search for potential models.

Being a customer of both Staples and Office Depot, she checked out their websites and was immediately attracted to a shiny red Sony Vaio that was available at each store. The fact that it was Sony, she says, did reassure her that this would be an excellent choice, based on the brand's reputation for quality, and her previous experience with other Sony products.

> *What's important to realize, as someone who is developing or marketing a brand, is that you may not be aware of your clients' or customers' buying styles.*

She decided to visit Staples first, since it was more convenient, but she was disappointed to learn that, while they had the Sony Vaio model she was looking for in stock, it was not available in red. However, the salesperson at Staples described all of the Vaio features, and its advantages over some of the other comparable laptops. The more she investigated, the more she became convinced to purchase this model.

She entered the store as a Trendsetter, looking for style and uniqueness, but as she became more involved, the Investigator took over and she began to ask more questions about features, warranties, memory, accessories, and of course, price. The more she learned, the less the color was a factor.

At this point, her Coordinator Style was putting together a mental list of what was most important to her in a laptop, and how she could network the laptop to the desktop at her office. She also considered how this model, more lightweight than others, would be easy to travel with, and could help her with her presentations. She was also pleased to see a model that was available in a silver "faux" alligator cover, which appeared to be more durable. It wasn't RED, but it still was stylish - and different!

Office Depot was still on her list, but the Staples associate took the time to explain all the laptop's features, benefits, and warranty options, and asked her how she was going to use it. Then he mentioned that if she didn't like it or it didn't live up to her expectations, she could bring it back to him within two weeks - with no arguments or hassles. He explained the significance of the extended warranty - even if she

dropped the computer, the laptop would be replaced. And, on top of that, he gave her a lower, unadvertised price that was better than several other brands in this store, or in any other store. What a deal!

The Relater Style was now convinced that no other searching was necessary. The Staples customer service was excellent, and this store was her best choice. She now had a "new best friend" at Staples - something every Relater values.

Was that it? No, it wasn't. After she took the laptop home, she noticed some scratches on the bottom that resulted from removing the bolts from the Staples shelf. The store manager offered to exchange it for a "fresh" laptop at another Staples store that was 2 hours away - where he happened to be going to attend a manager's meeting the next day. Her Trendsetter and Relater Styles were at the maximum satisfaction level (her most dominant preferences), and she felt comfortable that her Investigator and Coordinator styles were satisfied as well.

Each of her buying styles kicked in at different times, and as each one made its contribution, Staples become her preferred place to shop…a store to tell her colleagues about over the next several months.

There is no single box in which your buying style fits, because few people rely solely on one style. However, a hierarchy of dominance prevails, and you will most often make buying decisions based on the preference with the loudest voice - the one that has continued to wear a path in your brain buying the same things in the same way.

What's important for you to realize, as someone who is developing or marketing a brand, is that you may not be aware of your clients' or customers' buying styles. This creates the necessity for a brand that appeals to *all* buying styles. Your brand, including its features,

benefits, marketing materials, and Internet presence, need to feed the buying styles of whoever looks its way. How? Through the BrainBranding process.

A Guide to Optimizing the Four Buying Styles

As you continue to reflect on the four Buying Styles, keep the following points in mind. Each buying style is motivated by different factors in making a purchasing decision and, additionally, there are ways to communicate with each of the styles that will (1) gain their attention, (2) maintain their attention, and (3) move a prospect or potential buyer to take action.

Buying Style	Brand Motivators	Best Ways to Communicate
Investigator	• Competitive pricing • Positive bottom-line impact • No-frills products & services • Internet presence	• Provide facts and figures • Use logical assertions • Be accurate and clear • Be brief and concise
Coordinator	• Practicality of product/service • Reliable, dependable features • Organized presentation • Solving a business problem	• Begin with brand details • Discuss history & what preceded • Take a linear, sequential approach • Stay focused on topic

RELATER ♡	• Personalized service • Follow-on contact • Creating emotional connection • Friendly, no-pressure interactions	• Begin with small talk • Keep discussions open & informal • Demonstrate brand benefits • Illustrate points with stories
TRENDSETTER	• State-of-the-art brand concept • Original marketing strategies • Long-term brand value • Creative, cutting-edge design	• Begin with the big picture • Brainstorm ideas and possibilities • Be willing to move from topic to topic • Illustrate points with visual examples

CHAPTER 3:

BRAINBRANDING - MERGING BRAIN AND BRAND

Now that you're aware that your thinking processes and buying styles influence your purchasing decisions, you might ask, "How does this change the way I develop my brand strategy?" Or you might even question, "How is this relevant to my marketing strategy?"

You'll recall what we said in the introduction of this book: that while we came from two completely different disciplines, we discovered a tremendous amount of synergy between branding and the brain. Considering the fact that marketers seek to influence the brands you select, it should come as no surprise that there are parallels between *consumer buying behavior* and the *brain's buying preferences* used in making those decisions.

Your Brand's DNA

It's important to think about your brand in physiological terms since, as we believe from our research and experience, your brand makes up the DNA of your product, service, or company.

A body's DNA determines one's whole being: it's what differentiates you from all of the other people in the world, both physically and psychologically. Your DNA is your own chemical fingerprint, and understanding what makes you tick certainly can help you to be successful.

The same is true for a product or service (or yourself). A knowledgeable marketer must determine that your brand is your DNA - *before* trying to reach the potential client or customer base. The focus needs to be on defining and describing the DNA of the product: what makes it different, what makes it better, what appeals to the target consumer.

This is no small step in marketing your brand - in fact, it's the foundation for it. By going through the BrainBranding process, you can determine the likelihood of success and the potential for growth before you even begin to communicate its benefits and selling points.

If a company or marketer fails to recognize the importance of this description of the brand - its DNA - the chance for success is almost non-existent. And here's a critical point:

> *Since your brand is the DNA of your product/store/service, it forms the nucleus for all the decisions in moving the business, personal brand, or individual forward on the path to success.*

So let's begin to examine our brand strategy process. It's one that we've developed from many years of experience in working with diverse companies, individuals, as well as advertising agencies that recognized the importance of the brand in overall business success.

Based on our research, we believe that an effective brand strategy results from a two-phase approach:

- **Phase One: Brand Development**
- **Phase Two: Brand Implementation**

Unfortunately, many people go directly to Phase Two without taking the time to properly develop a strategy that reflects the entire organization's thinking, one that has the information to make implementation less risky and more effective. Why? Well, particularly in retailing, marketing is always under the gun for quick fixes and programs that can be implemented fast enough to demonstrate positive results before the next fiscal year, analyst's meeting, or annual report.

The question usually is: "How fast can we get this out to the consumer?" or "How much will this cost us and do we have the budget to make it happen fast?" The better question is: *"What is the right thing to do in order to make our brand stand out from the competition, and in such a way that we will have more clients, more trial purchases, and ultimately more sales and profits?"*

The answer to this question requires a systematic progression, one that consists of four steps (remember that there are four, since they coincide with the four Buying Styles). These steps must be executed in sequence in order to gain the maximum effectiveness in positioning your brand in the consumer's mind - and wallet.

> *What is the right thing to do in order to make our brand stand out from the competition?*

PetSmart - "Where Pets Are Family"

Making Branding a Priority

PetSmart, one of the country's largest and most successful chains of pet supplies, is a good example of finding the right branding solution. At one time, the company was growing, but had not differentiated itself from similar competitors, or even the major discount and food chains that were expanding their pet departments. (Note: When Ken was named their SAP-Marketing and Branding, they needed a new brand strategy - and the CEO wanted it fast!)

They formed a Brand Strategy Development committee to build their brand and then "sell" it within the company. It was decided that the entire organization had to be represented on the committee because the future success of the company was dependent on the work that the committee was about to produce.

And they were successful. Everyone was committed and quickly agreed on the major issues and differentiators that would bring about the success that was necessary - for all committee members. All these years later, even with several management changes along the way, the company continues to be the industry leader, and the essence of the brand has sustained because it was truly a team effort, one that included representatives from each of the four buying styles.

True Organizational Effectiveness

It's important to make sure that all types of thinkers and buying styles are represented when branding, because clients and customers are diverse, and they will be influenced in different ways when making brand selections.

In examining your brand's relationship with clients or customers, the following graphic illustrates why the four Buying Styles need to be taken into account: each one has a different focus, and each focus is essential to the BrainBranding process.

Merging Brain, Brand, and Buying Styles

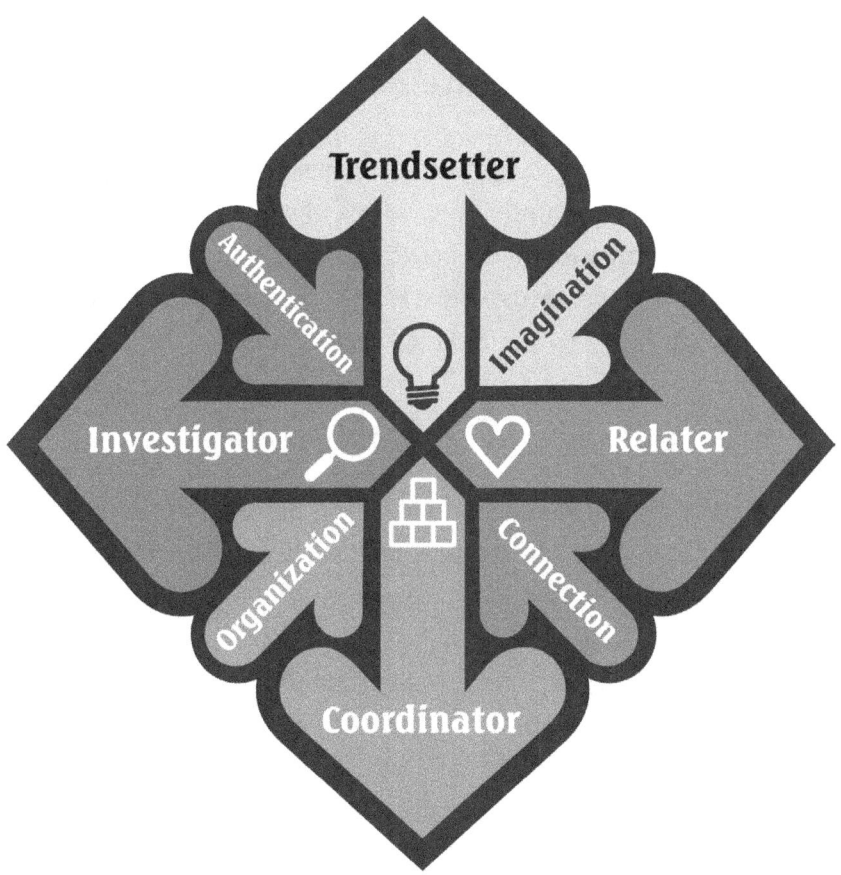

Authentication - The Truth of the Brand

This part of your brain is focused on the facts about your product or service. A retailer, for example, will need to be sure that the customer knows the facts about the store, what it sells, how many branches it has, how long it's been in business, its pricing. Facts, however, only describe WHAT you do.

Organization - The State of the Brand

This is where planning takes place. This part of your brain needs a step-by-step tactical plan that provides a blueprint for working with the buyer - one that is well structured and practical. This is the part of the brain that wants to know HOW you will take them - as a client or customer - to the next successful step.

Connection - The Heart of the Brand

It is here that an emotional bond is forged between your brand and your target client or customer, one that forms an enduring long-term relationship. It may be a customer service commitment, or a relationship marketing program that rewards the client/customer for his or her loyalty. Or it may mean supporting community events or charitable organizations. It establishes WHOM the connection is made with, and the tone that you use to communicate with the people who use your products and services.

Imagination - The Future of the Brand

This part of your brain requires a visionary element, one that provides the type of innovation and creativity that puts your brand on the cutting edge of business. For consumers seeking the latest in technology, ideas, or just plain know-how, your brand needs to ask this question: WHY is this the best brand to provide new, unusual experiences that differentiate it from your competitors - not just now, but in the future?

Now let's take a closer look at the Development Phase, and Step One of the BrainBranding process: **Create Your Vision**.

PHASE ONE: BRAND DEVELOPMENT

CHAPTER 4

BEGIN WITH THE BRAND IN MIND

STEP ONE - CREATE YOUR VISION

BrainBranding is the solution for developing a brand that has the ability to appeal to a greater number of people, and to have greater staying power with those people.

So how do you begin? We've developed a 4-step process that blends the Buying Style mentality with innovative branding and marketing strategies. The result? A brand that resonates with people even beyond your target market - one that leaves a positive, indelible impression.

Step One begins with a Visionary Outlook. Why? Because before you begin, you need to have a Vision: of your brand, your company, and the direction you want to take it into the future. You may remember Stephen Covey's book, *First Things First*, in which he says, "Begin with the end in mind." So in this step, you look ahead to the future, imagine your brand, consider why it has a reason for being, and what makes it unique in the marketplace.

> *Stephen Covey says, "Begin with the end in mind."*

So often people begin the branding process without a clear idea of what their objective is. It's not unlike having a map and not knowing what your final destination will be. There are many roads that you can take, but none of them will get you to the right place until you define where you want to end up.

What Does "It" Look Like?

Whether you're an entrepreneur, employee, or someone in between, it's important to have a clear picture of what you do, how you do it, and the people you want to influence to buy your products, services, ideas and concepts.

Completing the following sentence will give your brand definition a head start:

I'm not just a _____. I'm a
_____
who _____
_____.

Here's an example. A client of ours, a graphic artist, is highly conceptual and creative. She works with her own clients to develop marketing concepts and materials. Her work is beautiful and elegant, but she was perceived as not having her eye firmly planted on the bottom line. As we worked with her, we discovered that that was not the case at all. In fact, here's how she decided to describe herself:

> *"I'm not just a graphic artist: I provide designs that communicate bottom-line value - and results - to **my** clients, and to **their** clients."*

Her business:

> *Kate Sanborn Graphics: Designed to*
> *Communicate, Designed to $ell*.

The change in Kate's branding strategy pointed out to her clients and prospects that she was a businessperson first, and not only someone who was artistic and creative.

The Vision for *your* business will contain certain elements that, when they come together, are the beginning stages of formulating your brand. Here is a list of questions to help you begin:

- What are you selling?
- Who's in your target market?
- What are your specific area(s) of expertise?
- How do you like to work (alone, in teams, within a larger organization)?
- Does your business provide primary, secondary, or passive income?
- What revenues are you projecting?
- What are your deliverables?
- What is the size of your company/number of employees?
- What are your long- and short-term objectives?

What is Your Mission?

The mission of your brand is a critical element because it defines your purpose and objective. Do all the people connected with your brand agree on the mission? This is important if you and your business are going to live up to the brand.

The mission has to be your creed - and that of your company - because it affects every decision made within your organization. What will it look like as it evolves? And where does it end?

APPLE - "Think Different"

Steve Jobs, founder of the Apple brand, had a vision for his company that has remained a constant since its inception. That vision was challenged when Jobs became seriously ill and had to temporarily step away from the business. However, the company survived and continued to be a model in groundbreaking technology, because of the vision he had for Apple and his commitment to innovation and breakthrough ideas for the brand.

Apple's vision is built on the latest advances in technology, with products that set the standard not only for the company, but for the industry. It started with the first Macintosh PC and has grown consistently since then. Even with the failure of the Newton PDA early on, the company was recognized as cutting edge, and it created a nearly cult following that kept a loyal - though comparatively small - customer base.

Apple continued to innovate and stay a step ahead of the trends with new products like the iPod, the Mac Book, the iPhone, the iTouch and now the iPad. Product introductions rivaled the latest Hollywood releases for excitement and interest.

The niche that was originally created has now expanded to a mass audience who see Apple as the standard for high tech products and lifestyles to match. Illustrating Apple's increasing popularity, it sold 2 million iPads in the first two months following

its introduction. In comparison, it took the iPhone over a year to sell its first million units, and the iPod nearly two years to reach that plateau.

Steve Job's vision also led to the launch of the Apple Store. Now considered a phenomenon in the retail industry - even during a downturn in the economy - Apple stores bring the same look of originality that the products are known for, and they added the personal (emotional) contact that purchasers need and want. Programs such as One-to-One assistance to help with any questions and transitions from the PC world, and the Genius Bar that quickly takes care of any glitches or technical issues (usually human failures), bring the brand to life and create a loyalty - and packed stores - unmatched in retail today.

Apple created a personality, not just a brand - one that not only appeals to people who are creative and want to be on the cutting edge, but one that also appeals to all types of buying styles.

Your vision has to coincide with the benefits that your clients and customers are looking for. In Chapter 4, we'll explore their thinking in more depth, to see what the real behavioral motivators are that drive them to select one product, one store, or one service as their brand of choice.

In the case of developing a personal brand within your work environment, management is motivated by a number of factors in deciding who will move up to the next level of responsibility. A well-developed personal brand can help to fast track your career. Here's an example.

Herb Alpert/A&M Records

Herb Alpert was one of the top recording artists of the 60s and 70s. With his unique trumpet style and band, the Tijuana Brass, his music was not only some of the most identifiable, but also some of the most listened to during an era of free-spirited rock 'n roll (which sounded nothing like his signature songs).

Herb was popular internationally as well as domestically, and he even had a hit vocal solo ("This Guy") as well as his own weekly TV variety show. At the peak of his career, however, Alpert decided to rebrand himself in the recording industry when he formed a partnership with Jerry Moss and founded A&M records.

The A&M label became legendary for developing more musical stars than any label in recording history, and Alpert's direction and personal guidance led to the success of the company, as well as many of its individual performers. His rebranding plan differentiated A&M from others in the highly competitive music business: he and Moss developed a strategy that worked; it never really played on his previous celebrity, but rather on the industry expertise that he had cultivated over the years.

Eventually, A&M was sold to Polygram, one of the industry giants, and Alpert once again rebranded himself - this time as a teacher and philanthropist in the arts (especially music). He also re-focused his energies to become a talented sculptor and painter, with his works selling commercially and exhibited nationally. Herb Alpert's success was the result of his awareness of industry trends and needs, and then utilizing that expertise to become successful - over and over again.

The same holds true for those of you who aren't big celebrities (yet), but who may want or need to reinvent yourself by developing a fresh personal brand.

Desired Future State

An effective way of "beginning with the end in mind" - as Covey so eloquently stated - is to determine your vision using the Desired Future State process. This approach, which has been used by many companies with strong brands, begins by clearly defining where you are (your current state), and then asking these types of questions:

> ➢ How do you compare with your competition?
> ➢ How are you perceived by the people in your target market?
> ➢ How do you see the business changing during the next 3-5 years?
> ➢ Where do you want the business to be in 3-5 years?

Here's how BP addressed those questions.

BP - "Beyond Petroleum"

BP Oil has become a household name as a result of the massive oil spill in the Gulf of Mexico in 2010. However, BP hadn't always been as well known, even though it was one of the largest oil companies in the world.

The company, then known as British Petroleum, was primarily involved with oil discovery, refining, and product development. In the late 1980s, the company devised a strategy to grow its brand

presence, not only within the oil industry, but with consumers throughout the world.

With a plan to reach its "Desired Future State" as one of the top oil producers and retailers, it set out with a method to establish a new brand that appealed to customers in its own industry, as well as on the main highways of the world.

To make the transformation, BP acquired a number of already segmented, regional petroleum brands, such as Amoco and Standard and Boron, to bring them new management with a fresh and consistent look in their retail operations and products.

BP rolled out this transition market by market, with a highly creative yet fact-based marketing campaign that launched a new era in petroleum retailing that successfully met the needs of present-day consumers.

BP also focused on the size and scope of its operations to build an awareness and trust of new customers all over the world. They adjusted to the changing marketplace and, at the same time, maintained a dominant presence in the behind-the-scenes exploration and refining business.

BP's response to the oil spill debacle has been another ingredient in that branding process: appealing to the environmentalists as well as the other businesses and individuals affected by this major crisis.

Desired Future State

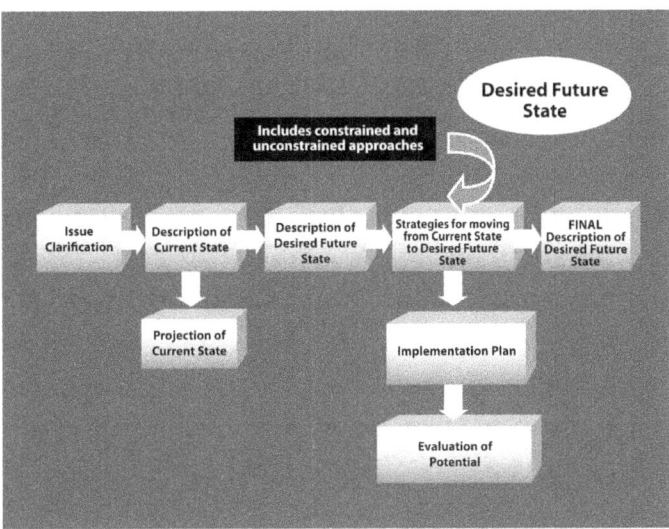

While creating your vision can be a mind-expanding experience that brings out the creativity in many people within the organization, it's important to consider the implications that will affect the development of a brand, and how they will take you to where you want to be.

Let's look at these through the Desired Future State process:

1. **Where are you Now?** The first three steps in the process are based on your assessment of where you and your brand currently are today, relative to the competition.

   • First, Issue Clarification is necessary to identify the barriers facing your success, or the growth of your current brand. These can be both external (e.g., the economy, fashion trends, media usage), or internal (e.g., company politics, reorganization). Whatever these factors may be, it's critical to spell out what they are and how they will

affect your brand's growth. Many brands fail to succeed because management chose to view the marketplace only through their own rose-colored glasses, and failed to realistically assess their position and/or potential.

- Second, you have to realistically define where your brand is positioned (if it currently exists) relative to the competition. A SWOT (Strengths, Weaknesses, Opportunities, and Threats) analysis is a wasted exercise if you don't understand your market share, consumer perception and preferences, and realistic assessment of your weaknesses, as well as your strengths, that need to be addressed in order to grow.

- Third, if nothing changes, you have to face the music and project where the brand will be in both the near and long-term, relative to the competition and in terms of market share and preferences.

   For example, Kodak realized that if they did not change their brand to reflect newer, emerging technologies and less photo development, the company would quickly lose its reason for being and its brand would lose most of its previously-dominant value to its customers (more on Kodak later).

2. **Describing your Future State.** Once you have a clear picture of where your brand stands, you can then create your preliminary vision for the brand. Describe the vision with specific enough details, so that you'll recognize it when you see it. To simply say "We want our brand to be a leader in its category" is not enough. That vision should detail where you want to be with your clients or customers, the competition, and market share.

Your future state is also the key to having a successful business plan. You have to be creative and innovative to describe the potential for your brand and what it can become - not only in financial returns, but also in the equity it will have with clients and customers in the future.

3. **Strategies to Get from Here to There.** Your strategies must reflect how your brand will stand out from the competition. What value will it provide that will differentiate your brand when it is presented to and then used by your buyers? How will you communicate these values in such a way that you create not just interest, but a genuine loyalty and "love" for your brand?

    Your marketing plans have to find that unique, creative, and empathetic way to say, "We know what you need. We know why you need it. And we'll help you to achieve the benefits of using our brand to meet that need." Then you can evaluate the real potential for success.

4. **Making Your Vision a Reality.** Once you have gone through the first steps of the process outlined above, then it's time to give form to your vision and what it will take to accomplish your goals. The vision you've defined is critical and must be understood by all within the organization, so that there is consistency and understanding of every move you make to reach the desired outcomes.

As you can see from the above discussion, the Desired Future State process requires that you succinctly define what is likely to happen if you don't change your current state. And then, finally, you need to

make an initial attempt - in writing - to determine where you want to be in the future (making your vision a reality).

The intermediate steps follow the brand development stage in our strategy; the key is to define each step and its impact while communicating with and getting input from all relevant people and functions. With this process, a brand can lay the groundwork for success and, as Steve Jobs did with Apple, create a unique brand in a crowd of competitors.

When you begin the process of creating your vision, along with the outcomes you want to achieve, you'll be in the initial stages - and the first step - of the BrainBranding process.

Red Roof Inn is an example of a company that systematically took the first step to achieving its Desired Future State. Let's examine how they changed their brand and improved their business.

Red Roof Inns - "Hit the Roof"

Changing the Brand for the Future

Several years ago, Red Roof Inns were one of many hotel chains competing in the economy segment of the hospitality industry. The chain had done well in establishing awareness of its brand, but the segment was getting more crowded with lower-end hotel chains that promised a less expensive price for a room. Red Roof Inns followed the Desired Future State process to determine a strategy to break away from the crowd, as follows:

- **Issue clarification**: This segment of the hotel industry was becoming increasingly competitive with Days Inn,

Super 8, and EconoLodge among the many chains that were competing for the traveler whose choice of brand selection was based on getting the lowest price, and who were willing to sacrifice some of the amenities to get it.

At the same time, business travelers (a more profitable customer base) were expecting higher quality and more convenience while still being cost conscious. It was becoming increasingly difficult to maintain revenues and grow profitability, as there was little differentiation among the brands in this segment.

- **Description of Current State:** Market Share continued to decline and brand awareness stagnated. Reservation lines (then primarily an 800 phone center) were not generating much interest or revenue. The brand had little distinction or loyalty among its targeted customers.

- **Projection of current state**. Not optimistic. The chain expected reservations to decline and, along with it, revenues and profits. Market share would continue to dwindle at an increasing rate.

- **Preliminary Desired Future State.** Red Roof realized that it had to move up to the next segment - budget lodging - in order to differentiate itself. It wanted to become the preferred choice of the cost-conscious business traveler. Finally, it wanted to increase brand preference by generating more online/800 reservations via its 1-800-theroof reservations center.

- **Strategies and Plans to move to the Desired Future State.** The entire organization needed to embrace

the upgrading - even though some were only slight modifications - in order to become a preferred choice of a broader customer base. In addition to upgrading the physical appearance and quality of the inns, Red Roof also improved the service and amenities.

Once these goals were accomplished, the chain aggressively marketed the reasons for choosing its brand over both the higher quality hotels (no frills that add to the rate) and the aggressive price-driven economy segment (better quality that you don't pay for).

Their communications were also consistently punctuated with a message driving reservations to the 800 call center: non-traditional messages in non-traditional media with memorable and consistent creative execution to differentiate and build more top-of-mind awareness.

- **Evaluation of Potential.** As the chain rolled out the new strategies in test markets, it evaluated and adjusted messages based on the feedback they received. The results were positive - increased awareness by double-digit percentages and increased business travel driven by significant increase in 800 direct reservations by more than 20%.

Red Roof Inns managed to maintain their low price image while now competing for the travel dollars from those who normally stayed at only moderate-priced chains. Despite greater pressure on travel budgets within corporations, Red Roof capitalized on the trend by using a commonsense approach that corporate controllers could understand and justify.

The company then knew where its future state would be and where they would achieve the growth and profitability necessary to maximize its potential. It didn't raise its sights too high, but just high enough to differentiate itself from both lower priced and higher priced alternatives. As you can see, it didn't happen by accident. It began with a vision that was well developed and well communicated.

Creating a Vision Appeals to the TRENDSETTER Buying Style

A brand that can be folded into a vision for the future - that is innovative and original - is important if your brand is going to appeal to the Trendsetters. They are looking for a state-of-the-art brand, and want to know how your brand will help them to achieve their future goals.

They also want assurance that they are perceived as being on the cutting edge in their choice of products and services, just as their personal vision determines their lifestyle and buying behaviors.

Trendsetters want to know where your brand is headed in terms of applications to their life or business that will positively affect them in the months and years to come. Your brand needs to demonstrate how you've captured their imagination and their dreams, i.e. where they want the direction of their lives and experiences to be heading. They are willing to take risks in the name of innovation, confident that your brand will fulfill their dream of a better future.

Beginning the BrainBranding Process

Here is an opportunity to launch the development of your brand, beginning with the first step of the BrainBranding process. Using the following chart, begin to Create your Vision.

DEVELOPING YOUR BRAND WORKSHEET
STEP ONE: CREATE YOUR VISION

The first step in the BrainBranding process is to develop a Vision for your brand. Complete the items below to begin the process of developing or re-creating your own brand (individual, business, or entrepreneurial).

1 Describe the **Vision** for your brand.

_____
_____
_____
_____

2 What do you want to be famous for with your client and customers?

_____
_____
_____
_____

3 Describe your personal, or business, mission.

_____
_____
_____
_____

4 What would happen if you didn't create a Vision statement for your brand?

_____
_____
_____
_____

5 What is the desired future state for your brand?

_____
_____
_____
_____

6 How does your brand activate the brain of the Trendsetter Style?

_____
_____
_____
_____

CHAPTER 5

IF IT'S NOT FACTUAL, IT'S NOT ACTUAL

STEP TWO - CONDUCT RESEARCH

Step Two in the BrainBranding process reflects **Investigator** thinking. It's here that you will need to gather facts, conduct research, and perform comparative analyses between your business and those competing with you. How is your brand (or company) the same or different from the competition? What will differentiate you? Who are your buyers? Are you state-of-the-art or so last century?

Why Research?

Research is essential to your success; otherwise you might be spending time and money without any tangible payoff. Research gives you the advantage of anticipating the questions that people will ask, and having the answers.

You simply need to research the information that will help you determine your market situation and business trends. After that, you may determine that there are still some questions that need to be answered, or some other variables that need to be studied.

This will require proprietary research that you and your company will need to field, compile, and analyze to gain the information and direction that you need. In other words, you are the primary source of these studies and the information is exclusive to your needs.

Secondary Research

For those who are the Coordinator style, don't be confused by the order of this discussion. Secondary research is not the second phase of your investigative activities. In this step, secondary means that the information comes from *secondary sources,* and from data that already exists.

There's a wealth of information that relates to your product category, your market, and your competition. Many trade associations and publications conduct annual surveys of their industry that provide current trends and data. This information can be extremely valuable in making decisions about your brand's viability and position. Searches on Google and other similar services provide information almost immediately that is specifically tailored to your market situation.

Suppliers and consulting firms also conduct objective research that is available to companies (that is, not proprietary) and that can be instrumental in making the decisions necessary to validate your vision and determine your current position relative to the competition.

Primary Research

When the data you need isn't readily available, then you'll need to go out and ask the right questions directly. There are a number of ways to gather information:

Focus groups can provide qualitative insights on the perceptions and feelings that customers have toward your product or service. These groups are also valuable as sounding boards to test new concepts and ideas, and to prevent investing a lot of time and money on an initiative that may sound good, but simply doesn't resonate with your buyers.

Exit interviews are another valuable survey technique, especially for retailers. There is no better way to get spontaneous, qualitative data on why customers shop in your stores than by asking them as they leave the store. You can determine why they came in, what they were looking for, what else they purchased, and why they didn't buy what they came in for. If service is a problem, you'll find out quickly from customers who are honest when it comes to their behaviors when they are on the spot.

Telephone interviews have been the mainstay for consumer research for years and can provide significant, quantitative data. However, it can take some time to obtain and analyze the results.

Online surveys are currently the most used; they not only provide accurate data, but they also provide the data in real time, making the analysis much more timely.

There are other techniques that can be reliable as well - the best course of action is to work with a professional research firm and

clearly define (1) what information you are trying to gather, and (2) what decisions will be made as a result of analyzing that data.

Who are your primary clients and customers, and how do they feel about your brand? What are their likes and dislikes? What do they want or need, given the changes in today's economy? And finally, you have to research the market to understand what trends or innovations will affect your business in both the short and long term.

With this knowledge, you can then revise, improve, change (or even cancel) your plans to move forward. Today's technology affords you the opportunity to get the right information faster and more specifically than ever before. Participation and statistically significant information is more attainable for less money. Conducting Research is a critical step and, even if there is a great deal of existing data, you have to remember that the market is changing faster than ever before, so the facts need to be recent and accurately analyzed.

Most important, don't forget to research the people most connected to your brand or business to determine how they feel about your brand and what they know that could affect your vision.

What about a personal brand strategy? The same need for research holds true for an individual brand. While there may not be quantitative data available, it's still important to talk with your peers, your friends, your family, and your boss to determine just where you stand.

You may be surprised at the number of strengths you have, what you are famous for, and what your value is, and you can determine all of these with candid, honest conversations with the people who

know you best. A personal SWOT analysis is critical here to help you grow and maximize your potential.

Here's how conducting research made a significant difference in revitalizing and expanding the Home Depot brand.

Home Depot - "You Can Do it, We Can Help"

A Retail Brand Story

Home Depot has been successful almost since it was founded in 1978 by Arthur Blank and Bernie Marcus. Its growth and the commitment of its people are legendary. However, a few years ago, soon after the founders retired, the company began to lose market share and saw sales become sluggish for the first time in its history. They could have blamed the economy (which wasn't so bad at that time) or they could have blamed the aggressiveness of Lowe's marketing. But they didn't.

Home Depot chose to conduct additional research, and one of their findings was that a primary customer was a "she"- not a "he" - and that more than 40% of their sales were to female shoppers. Yet, their store was designed mostly for the handyman, and their marketing revolved more around sports than home fashion, which was becoming an important part of their business.

With those facts in hand, Home Depot now knew that their customer had changed, and they knew what she needed and wanted. So they revamped the appliance selection and expanded and redesigned their kitchen remodeling department. And they added more women to their staff - at both the store level and in their Atlanta home base.

They launched extra in-store seminars and displays to help their new customer learn how to design her home the way she wanted it. These were called "Do-It-Herself" workshops, and the company marketed them with a multi-media campaign that spoke her language, with features and promotions that she was interested in.

The company soon began to bounce back and regained some lost market share - all because Home Depot took the time to get the facts first. Then they moved forward aggressively with their vision for the company, which ultimately became the third largest retailer in the world.

A Personal Brand Story

Now here's an example of how research helped to redefine and revitalize the business of one of our clients, Charles Davies. Charles was a successful entrepreneur, well known for providing exhilarating learning experiences during his training programs. But in a changing economy, he realized that that wasn't enough.

Client surveys and other research tools that Charles used indicated that his clients were looking for their investment to have long-term staying power, both intellectually and emotionally. He determined that providing the potential for future change within the organization was what his clients were seeking. Here's how he decided to describe himself:

> "I'm not just a trainer: I'm a facilitator who ensures your training investment today - for success tomorrow."

His business:

Charles Davies - Innovative Learning Design
Engage the Mind…Retain the Knowledge
…Involve the Heart

Before, Charles had "work." Now he has a personal brand that will be a great help to both him and his clients in defining and differentiating his work as a trainer. He presents himself as a business person who understands his clients' businesses, which is a valuable asset in his competitive market.

CarMax - "The Way Car Buying <u>Should</u> Be"

Find Out What They Don't Like

CarMax has changed not only the way people buy used cars, but has also changed the industry along the way. They do things much differently from other dealers who line the main streets across America.

The reason they do things so differently is the result of a great deal of research, which they conducted even before they opened their first showroom and car lot. What they needed to know was what people *didn't like* about the typical used car purchase experience - and then change it. For example, people said they didn't like to negotiate the price, and they never really believed the price on the window or in the ad, so CarMax set a policy where the price that was posted was the price that was paid. Period.

Sales were not made by salespeople. In their place were friendly, helpful professionals whose job was to help you find the car that

met your needs and wants, not try to hammer out the best deal. No commissions. No bait and switch tactics. Instead, there was a buyer-friendly system that showed the cars, their prices, their features, the facts. Trade-ins weren't traded. Instead, you could bring your car in and have a professional appraiser examine it and give you the price the company would pay for it (whether you bought another car from CarMax or not). All the information that a buyer needed without the hassle.

In addition, the showrooms were child-friendly. Understanding that more than half of their purchasers were women, the buying experience became more appealing to women: the sales staff was more than 50% women, and the surroundings included play rooms where kids could occupy themselves in a supervised environment while their moms checked out the inventory or took a test drive.

The result? Their research indicated which models their target customers preferred, and CarMax made sure that they had a larger-than-average selection of the Camrys, Accords, and Minivans that reflected what these customers wanted. CarMax created one the most successful innovations in the automotive industry in the last two decades. All as a result of listening to the customer first.

Princess Cruise Lines - "Escape Completely"

Determine What Motivates the Customer

Another key to executing the right brand strategy is to determine what motivates the customer to choose your product or service over the alternatives. Princess Cruise Lines is one of the largest companies in the leisure travel business, and for a very good reason.

Not only did they thoroughly research what people wanted and expected from a vacation cruise, but they also determined what would convince a traveler to take a cruise rather than fly to their destination. After all, it would seem to be a no-brainer to get where you wanted to go faster and more conveniently by taking an airplane (rather than spending several days on the water).

Princess decided to research what travelers *disliked* most about air travel, and they placed that information in an ad that highlighted their ships as a much more pleasurable alternative to the hassles of flying.

Picture this: They showed the discomfort of being in a center seat, next to a sweaty, food gobbling, sneezing passenger. They showed a rambunctious child in the seat directly in front of the passenger, a child who was screaming and jumping up and down to such a degree that it drove the passenger to consider bailing out at 30,000 feet.

Finally, Princess contrasted this craziness with the calm, relaxing atmosphere on the deck of one of their liners. Anybody who has ever flown - especially on a long-distance trip - can relate to the types of frustration they highlighted. A cruise was the logical alternative that offered what a traveler was looking for in a vacation. Aa-choo.

Conducting Research Appeals to the INVESTIGATOR Buying Style

Your research is all about uncovering facts - facts that will help you to make the decisions necessary to create a brand that resonates with your target clients and customers. The Investigator style wants you to provide them with the information that you have collected to develop your brand, so that they can make an intelligent buying decision.

Investigators want to know why your brand is a sound investment, particularly in comparison to the competition. How has it performed during the past five years? What about standards of quality? Why should they be loyal to your brand? How does it work, and what makes it tick?

They want information - including pricing - that will help them make an intelligent, rational decision, and they want to be able to stay on top of change through your Internet presence.

Developing Your Brand - the Second Step

Take a moment to reflect on the research that will make a difference in developing your brand. Complete the chart for Step Two of the BrainBranding process.

DEVELOPING YOUR BRAND WORKSHEET
STEP TWO: CONDUCT RESEARCH

Step Two in the process is to determine the type of Research you will need to conduct to make yourself and your brand contemporary and competitive. Complete the questions below to continue the process of developing your brand.

1 Who and what should you **Research** in relation to your brand's positioning, compared to you those who are vying for the same business?

_____
_____
_____
_____

2 What will make your brand more unique and competitive?

_____
_____
_____

3 How are your competitors' products or services similar to your brand?

_____
_____
_____
_____

4 How are your competitors' products or services different?

_____
_____
_____

5 How will you know your brand is successful?

_____
_____
_____

6 How does your brand activate the brain of the Investigator Style?

_____
_____
_____

CHAPTER 6:

MAKE A FRIEND FOR LIFE
STEP THREE: COMMUNICATE EMOTIONAL VALUE

Bill Bernbach, a well-known advertising guru, has said that people like to do business with people they like. **Step Three** of the BrainBranding process is about identifying the areas of personal connection for your prospects and clients, both internal and external. This step reflects the Relater Style, and it creates a way for people to have a long-term connection to you and your brand.

Step Three is what gives your brand staying power. Your brand needs to not only connect to your target market, but also become a resource that people can return to time after time, to ultimately become someone - or some thing - they can trust.

Although you may not realize it, as an individual, you are responding all the time to emotional stimuli - attending meetings, watching a TV show or movie, or talking with family members. From football games to family photos, people emote. How will they emote about *your* business, and about *your* brand?

We've talked about the importance of conducting research to unearth the facts that will help you define your product and its

position - objectively and realistically. Many feel that, armed with the facts, they can go out to the public and create brand messages that address the factual advantages or disadvantages. The result? They may be building awareness, but may be lacking emotional involvement. In other words, they appeal to the head, but not to the heart.

As you can see in the chart below, an effective brand must present both the TRUTH of your product or service and, at the same time, provide an emotional connection - or the HEART of the brand.

To have a sustainable brand with your client or customer, you must form a contract that includes not only the facts, but also a relationship that drives deep to the emotions of each person you are trying to influence, thereby generating a positive feeling about what you're offering. It's this marriage of Truth and Heart that creates an enduring relationship and a successful brand.

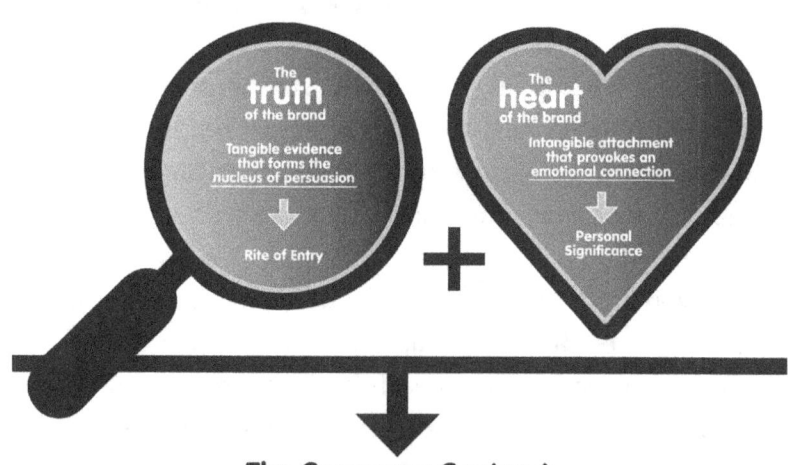

The Consumer Contract
The foundation of a preemptive and enduring relationship

Consider some of the brands that you feel strongly about - the ones that you return to - time after time. Is it a type of car, a line of clothing, a particular store? In fact, without a relationship or something or someone to respond to, you simply have no brand. So, armed with a vision for your brand and the facts to show that it is viable and can be differentiated, you're ready to get to the "HEART" of your brand.

This is the time to make an emotional connection with your clients or customers, so that you are not just another brand, but a person with whom they have established a relationship. And that relationship must create a positive feeling or experience, one that builds brand preference and loyalty.

Think about it this way. Take an imaginary (or actual) walk through the mall and notice the store signs as you pass by. Some will immediately register a feeling that will help you decide whether to enter or walk on by. Others (many others) will just be signs, and not conjure up any recognition or feelings. Why? Because you have no emotional connection to the store.

Connecting with people requires a brand strategy that resonates with the brain's natural motivators - the ones from the four Buying Styles. You have to make sure that you - and your brand - provide memorable experiences, where people walk away feeling smart and satisfied. You have to add meaning to their life in a way that makes them feel good about your brand and good about themselves for selecting it.

> *There are thousands of brands that people are aware of, but the key is to have an inner connection that creates positive feelings about your brand.*

Making the Right Connection

How do you forge a long-lasting, emotional connection? One of the best tools we've seen is the benefit ladder, which probes into the true motivation behind purchases. Below is the example of a benefit ladder for a pet store.

RETAIL PET STORE

The key is to start at the bottom of the ladder and enumerate the immediate benefits for selecting your product or service, or shopping in your store. These benefits often coincide with the "truth" of the brand, and are easily identifiable.

As you work your way up the ladder, identify the multiple benefits that come from those on the lower rung. You continue to work your way up until a deeply personal motive is uncovered. In this case, the most personal benefit is that shopping at this pet store

will make you feel like a good person who cares about your family, which includes your pets.

Once the Retail Pet Store determined that their target customers treated their pets as family members, it was much easier to probe into the real motivations - or benefits - that brought customers to their store and kept them loyal. Their branding strategy was based on a personal connection and how the experience made the customers feel about themselves for shopping at this store.

Many organizations believe that, by producing creative commercials or advertisements, they can connect with their people in an emotional way. Dream on. They forget that people connect to other people, and failing to forge those relationships can result in lost business.

A Personal Brand Story

One of our clients, Pam Smythe, approached us with a challenge. As a marketing manager in a financial services organization, Pam was looking to develop an "internal" brand that would get her more recognition with senior management. They had witnessed her creative side, but not her analytical side.

As a motivational leader, Pam prided herself on performance excellence while empowering and inspiring those around her. Yet she knew she needed to demonstrate a different side to her work persona. Here's how she decided to describe herself:

> *"I'm not just a marketer: I'm a marketing professional who leads others to produce bottom-line business results."*

Her brand:

Getting Down to Business, One Person At a Time.

While Pam's background and experience were in the marketing sector, she needed to be perceived as a bottom-line person as well. She began by writing articles for the company newsletter about the link between marketing campaigns and increases in revenue; then she spearheaded internal conferences that gave her additional visibility, and she was on her way.

FedEx - "The World - On Time"

FedEx is a great example of communicating emotional value. They have set the standard for overnight delivery throughout the world. But if it were just delivering packages, the company would not continue to be strong in today's economy.

When FedEx started out, there were already other overnight delivery options available. So here was the opportunity: when people needed to send something overnight, it was generally accompanied by a sense of urgency - in other words, emotion. The package just *had* to get there. It was important. And people needed to trust that FedEx would deliver on their promise.

FedEx built their company on this trust factor: they, unlike their competition, would absolutely, positively get it there when their customers needed it to arrive. And this commitment was demonstrated in every aspect of their business - from their hub in Memphis to the drop box in front of your building. Most of all, it would be present in the people who made it all happen.

The stories of FedEx employees going above and beyond to get the package delivered became so legendary that the movie *Castaway*, with Tom Hanks, was built around that commitment, and was later used in one of their TV spots. Most important was that this philosophy was communicated every day through the people who drove their trucks, as well as those in the drop-off centers, in the air, and on the highway.

Today, people continue to trust Fed Ex more than any other delivery service. Why? Because FedEx made an emotional connection with their customers and delivered on their promise. They still do.

Jimmy Carter - Getting the Vote For Your Favorite Brand

Political races are won or lost by the degree to which candidates have been able to connect emotionally to their constituents before election day. In 1980, not many "experts" believed that Jimmy Carter had a chance to win his party's nomination, much less win the election for the presidency of the United States. The fact that he had small-town roots in rural Georgia was just one of many reasons that not many voters had a connection with this candidate.

Because he was a relatively unknown governor from a southern state, most of the media was centered on "Who is this guy?" and not much on "What does he stand for?" Carter decided to make this his

strength as his campaign took off, building a brand that was based on his small-town image and his honest, straightforward personality. He used these characteristics to "connect" to a population that was looking for these traits, following several years of politicians not living up to the standards of the office.

Jimmy Carter became the "people's candidate," one who developed a strong following of those who believed he was an authentic person who would approach the office of the presidency in a realistic, down-home way, with family values and honest standards of responsibility.

And it worked. He surprised not only the Republicans, but also many in his own party, by building a brand that resonated with real people looking for someone they could connect with emotionally. Carter's brand has gone on to make him one of the most admired, influential people in the world, based on the foundation of his brand personality from many years earlier.

Eckerd - "America's Family Drug Store"

Before it was sold to JC Penney in the late 1990s, Eckerd Drugs was consistently the market share leader in the 15 states in which it operated stores. This was a result of aggressive marketing and geographical expansion, combined with excellent operational efficiency.

Eckerd made a commitment to ongoing research with its customers and its competitors. As more discount chains expanded to include pharmacies and lower prices, the company had to find more advantages than convenient locations. In addition, grocery chains expanded their offerings to include pharmacies and increased their

over-the-counter medications in order to make them more of a one-stop shopping experience.

What Eckerd discovered was that their customers were loyal to the pharmacists - and not to the pharmacies. And, it was their established personal relationships with consumers that kept them coming back, even when they could save more time and money by going to the other stores.

To build on those personal relationships, Eckerd consistently developed programs and promotions that encouraged direct contact between the pharmacists and the customers. One such program was developed in conjunction with SmithKline Diagnostics, including a local hospital in each market, and one of the network affiliate television stations in each Eckerd metro market.

The purpose of the program was to educate the public about colorectal cancer - then known as the "cancer nobody talks about" - and how important early detection is to preventing serious complications and death. The station's news departments did a weeklong series on the disease, and Eckerd practically gave away SmithKline's hemoccult testing kits (at a cost of one dollar each).

The hospital conducted the tests to determine any traces of blood for further examination. In the process, customers interacted with the pharmacists. The stations interviewed the pharmacists live during their reports, and the hospitals contacted the patients for personal follow up.

The results were better than encouraging. After distributing over a million kits each year, the collaboration discovered more than 600 positive cases of colon cancer, and saved several lives. And the results

for Eckerd? Professional respect of the pharmacists continued to grow based on the research studies conducted on consumers in each market. Furthermore, not only were pharmacists proud of their contribution to good health, but they also remained loyal to a company "that did this kind of program."

The emotional connection was best summed up by one patient who had surgery as a result of the testing program when he said, "I just thank God for Eckerd and Channel 8 for saving my life."

Target - "Expect More. Pay Less."

A Lesson in Building an Emotional Connection

Target stores - like many other discount chains - have always done major business with back-to-school merchandise, offered at exceptionally low prices. Similar to the other chains, Target promoted these items with advertising for major sale events, and their business continued to grow. However, Target was aware that it would take a personal connection with their customers to keep students and parents loyal - not just today, but for years to come.

They also knew that this loyalty would prove invaluable to their business - not just during this one season but throughout the year - since their research showed that low pricing was only one of many factors customers considered when selecting a store for their purchases.

Target believed that it could build its relationship by offering not just discount prices, but a percentage of its corporate profits to schools and charitable institutions in the markets where they operated.

They created an emotional connection by letting the customer choose who would get the benefit of their purchases. In doing so, not only did Target foster loyalty, but they also benefitted from the encouragement the schools and organizations gave their families to shop at Target, since it would benefit their programs with every dollar spent by the customers.

Their customers already knew that Target was a major company based in Minneapolis, but now they also knew that their local store was helping their schools as well. Give them high grades for this branding program!

An Emotional Connection Appeals to the RELATER Buying Style

We've emphasized that, unless your brand has a relationship with your customers, you have no brand. So what kind of relationship is the Relater seeking? It comes down to an emotional connection that you and your brand need to foster.

Bill Bernbach, one of the pioneers of the advertising agency business, talked about this when he encouraged his clients to take a stance with their customers:

> "If you stand for something, you will find some people for you and some against you. If you stand for nothing, you will find no one for you nor against you."

You can't please everyone, but the ones who build a genuine relationship based on something that is personally important to their buyers prove to have the most successful brands.

The relationship can be built on marketing messages that come from the heart, speaking to those emotions that move people. For example, it can be built on providing personalized customer service that goes beyond expectations and creates a response that leads to word-of-mouth, viral marketing. It can be reinforced by sponsorships that position the brand to be a good citizen of the community or supporter of charitable causes.

B.J. Bueno, the author of *Cult Branding*, encourages marketers to build a brand loyalty that is so strong that it takes much more than a competitive message or a better deal to motivate a customer to even consider another brand. Without that emotional connection, the brand is just there - on the shelves, in the mall, or sitting in an advertisement.

Relaters want to feel special, and will reward your brand with loyalty - by making it an important part of their business - and their life.

BrainBranding - The Next Step

Now you're ready for Step Three - communicating your brand's emotional value.

DEVELOPING YOUR BRAND - WORKSHEET
STEP THREE: COMMUNICATE EMOTIONAL VALUE

Step Three in the process is to create an emotional connection between your buyers and your brand. Complete the questions below to continue the process of developing your brand.

1 How will people **Connect Emotionally** to your brand?

_____
_____
_____
_____

2 Consider the Benefit Ladder: who will benefit most from your products or services?

_____
_____
_____
_____

3 In what ways will people benefit?

_____
_____
_____
_____

4 What qualities does your brand possess that will instill sustained loyalty?

_____
_____
_____
_____

5 What's the emotional value of your brand to clients and customers?

_____
_____
_____
_____

6 How does your brand activate the brain of the Relater Style?

_____
_____
_____

CHAPTER 7:

THE BRIDGE FROM BRAIN TO BRAND
STEP FOUR - CONSTRUCT A PLAN

We've reached the final step of the BrainBranding process. In Chapter 3, we described the four different ways that your brain chooses to focus when making a branding and/or buying decision. As we discussed previously, one of those focuses is "Organization - the State of the Brand." It's here that all your efforts come together: it's the part of the process that organizes the details about your brand and develops new marketing programs, which you will need to construct your plan.

It's in Step 4 that you combine (1) the vision and mission for your brand, (2) the research you conducted, and (3) the emotional connection to your clients and customers - into a focused, sustainable plan.

Several years ago, Simon and Garfunkel's first big song was "Bridge over Troubled Water" - a love song that pledges to help one's friend/lover to get through the tough times, just as a bridge helps one cross over to the safety of the other side of the river.

In much the same way, a brand that has a loyal following serves the same function: to help a company or individual over the slumps in

the economy, intense competition, or unforeseen problems, in its quest to achieve its vision. Just as this bridge needs to be structured to withstand the tides of adversity, the plan for communicating and executing the brand strategy must also be developed in such a way that it can be rolled out to all the people you are potentially targeting.

In this step, you will develop a brand and strategy that has structure, form, detail, and a targeted implementation plan. It's time to make sure that your brand will achieve preferred status with your clients, customers and prospects.

As we pointed out previously, people in today's business environment have a tendency to develop the plan and start executing it right away. Why? Because they want to see change and they want to see it immediately. However, the imperative here is that you have to go through Steps One through Three FIRST.

If you haven't established your brand's value, you'll be limiting your appeal to a lower number of clients and customers, and you'll be limiting your success as well.

Your plan has to take into account the brain's four buying styles to ensure that you are covering all the key factors that will hit home within and beyond your target market, and then make that plan work smoothly and efficiently.

Walmart - "Save Money. Live Better."

A Retail Brand Story

Walmart certainly knows what success means. And Sam Walton's plan for his company wasn't based solely on pricing. Low prices

were Walmart's foundation, but Sam - and his successors - knew that the plan had to go beyond just a markdown or sales promotion. They looked around at their competition and realized that accomplishing their goals required a plan that included their employees, their suppliers (who needed to do things differently to share in the success), their local communities (that would benefit from the increased business), and the additional employment that a really successful store would bring.

The plan was built on a vision to be the largest retailer in the world (now the largest company of any kind). To do this, they needed to look at the competition's weaknesses. Their research indicated that many discounters (e.g., Kmart) had low prices, but mostly on sale items - items that they quickly ran out of, resulting in disappointed customers.

So their plan dictated that there would be no sales - ever. No short-term promotional events. Just well stocked stores with items customers needed right away, and at really low prices. And the plan worked.

Next, they communicated the plan to their employees. In fact, their Saturday morning meetings are legendary. In addition, they represented the company's commitment to get everyone involved and sharing in what it would take to be successful. This philosophy was passed on at both the store and distribution center levels, where the people loved the company and loved their jobs.

Of course, there were some well-publicized exceptions (you can't expect perfection with more than a million employees and managers), but overall everyone bought in to the store's promise, and clearly it didn't happen by coincidence. Then, when everyone was on board, they began to communicate it to the customers.

Their ongoing, aggressive campaigns featured real customers, real associates, and real suppliers talking about a real store with a real plan. And the rest, as they say, is history.

A Personal Brand Story

Laura Baxter came to us with extensive experience as an HR generalist, which she felt was not sufficient to differentiate her expertise within the larger HR community. But her knowledge of Employee Relations law and HR liability was essential to many organizations.

We realized that Laura's strength lay as a business partner, where she would find specific applications for her generalist background. She would then be able to offer clients flexible solutions, and time- and money-saving procedures, while minimizing internal employee conflicts. Laura described her brand this way:

> *"I'm not just an HR professional: I'm a business partner who handles your people problems and keeps you from having more."*

Her business:

> **Baxter Consulting Group - Your Business Partner for HR Solutions**

Laura realized that one of her greatest assets was her ability to work within a client company's many departments and employees to formulate a plan for each of their challenges. She became much more than an outside consultant; her ability to solve problems using workable plans made her an invaluable partner, one that they called upon time after time.

Martha Stewart Living Omnimedia - "Sharing the Good Things Everyday"

Martha Stewart - Following Her Recipe for Success

In the past few years, Martha Stewart has re-emerged as one of the top brands in media, retail, and entertainment. Despite a period when her integrity and reputation came under intense scrutiny, Martha developed her brand even more strongly than before - across all channels, and among her target customers. How? It can be attributed to the characteristics that made her brand so successful initially, and what makes it so resilient today.

Martha Stewart's name has become affiliated with many different business ventures, through a well-developed plan. When she was a homemaker in Nutley, New Jersey, Martha published her first cookbook by amassing the details that she had accumulated through cooking in her own kitchen.

These were the traits that made her famous, and she and her brand became a household name, largely due to her organizational expertise - whether it was a recipe, a design for your home, instructions in making crafts, or her in her publications and television shows.

Martha had a step-by-step plan for success, implemented simply and personally by a woman whose brand continues to thrive.

Kodak - "Share Moments. Share Life."

Getting the Picture of a Changing Brand

One of the most powerful brands for more than a century has been Kodak. The name Kodak has been synonymous with quality photos for decades, and its market share has dominated the film and photo processing world.

Then the industry changed. Digital was changing the way we took and shared photos of our important memories. Analysts and retailers alike prognosticated the company's eventual demise, as fewer and fewer people used traditional film and processing. Picture taking, on which Kodak had built its brand, had changed dramatically, and the company would struggle to survive.

However, that didn't happen. Kodak changed its business model, and its consumer business has dramatically evolved to embrace a digital world. How did Kodak make this happen? It was all in the plan.

Kodak recognized the digital wave, long before it became the norm. As a result, it began changing its model by converting cameras to digital formats that not only were affordable, but that also competed favorably with the same quality as its former film and processing standards.

Kodak developed (no pun intended) one of the first on-line photo downloading and sharing programs to help its customers use digital photos to meet their personal needs. It produced a line of printers for the consumer market and photographic paper to match the exact needs of that market.

Today, Kodak continues to innovate and improve as this industry and technology change. But it wasn't luck that continued their profitability and success. The company developed (indeed!) a plan to capitalize on the new technology with a brand that maintained a strong tradition and a bright future.

How will you construct and implement a plan for your brand?

Constructing a Plan Appeals to the COORDINATOR Buying Style

One of the key factors in making a purchase decision today is convenience. This is the convenience of being able to find a location near home or online, and being able to find sufficient detailed information to help them make the right buying decision. For Coordinators, convenience also includes a brand that has ease of use, simple replacement, and organized directions on how to get the most from the purchase.

Coordinators are also interested in your brand's history, as well as the quality and reliability of your brand's products or services. Will they need service or replacement frequently? If you're a retail establishment, Coordinators are looking for an organized, well-signed, easily shopped environment.

In your marketing messages, Coordinators prefer detailed information in a systematic, step-by-step format that helps them determine how you can provide what they need. And they want to know how they will use or apply your brand to their business or life in a practical way.

Coordinators appreciate a well-targeted brand message; they seek out thoroughness and organization of information that will motivate them to come back to your brand - time after time.

The Final Step - Brand Completion

Putting together a plan for your brand is Step Four in the BrainBranding process.

DEVELOPING YOUR BRAND - WORKSHEET
STEP FOUR: CONSTRUCT A PLAN

During Step Four in the process you develop an implementation plan to set your brand into motion. Complete the questions below to conclude Phase One.

1 What elements do you need to include in your **Implementation Plan?**

_____
_____
_____
_____

2 What is your value proposition (what you offer to your clients and customers)?

_____
_____
_____
_____

3 What and who are your target markets?

_____
_____
_____

4 Who are the primary contacts in your networking process?

_____
_____
_____

5 What is the sequence in rolling out your plan?

_____
_____
_____

6 How does your brand activate the brain of the Coordinator Style?

_____
_____
_____
_____

Completing Your Brand - Putting it All Together

The final step in the BrainBranding process is to finalize your brand statement. Complete each of the steps below, and then put it all together in the space at the bottom.

1 The Vision for your Brand:

_____

_____

_____

_____

2 The Research for and Facts about your Brand:

_____

_____

_____

_____

3 The Emotional Connection to your Brand:

_____

_____

_____

_____

4 The Implementation Plan for your Brand:

_____

_____

_____

_____

Your Brand Statement:

PHASE TWO: BRAND IMPLEMENTATION

CHAPTER 8:

IMPLEMENTATION - BRINGING YOUR BRAND TO LIFE

Brand implementation represents Phase Two of the BrainBranding process, and it happens successfully when you've spent the time and energy necessary to make sure the first four steps are properly completed.

Now is the time to live up to the brand every day, at every level of the organization and in every function. And the key to a winning, ongoing implementation is communication from within.

A Typical Implementation Scenario

In an organization's marketing group, the focus all too often is on this phase first and, unfortunately, the developmental steps may not be given the attention or energy necessary to make sure that

Even more critical is getting everyone to participate in ensuring that the brand is implemented at every touch point - on a daily basis.

brand strategy resonates once the marketing rolls out to the organization and the customer.

Let's take a look at how the average company sets out to rebrand itself or its products and services. In the interest of expediency, they often miss some important foundation-laying steps that can assure success. Often driven by lagging sales or loss of market share, the company's senior management establishes a priority to "re-brand" its offerings. After some discussion (usually heated), the task is given to the marketing head to begin the process immediately and bring back some new brand thinking by a certain date (which is often very soon).

Knowing its charge, marketing gathers its troops together and explains the need and the urgency for the branding initiative. We say branding here, and they probably do as well, but often it's really a marketing/advertising focus.

The marketing staff, therefore, calls in their ad agency for some strategic discussions. If the pressure from senior management is strong enough, there may even be a decision to search for a new agency that will provide the "fresh thinking and objectivity" that the marketing group needs at this time.

Of course, such a conclusion usually delays the process even more, so often marketing will stick with its known entity (the current agency), so that there is no learning curve before moving forward. There will be several meetings, and perhaps some focus groups; then a new "ad campaign" will be presented. Sometimes, a revised positioning theme will be recommended as well, to demonstrate the new voice to the buyer. In reality, this is probably just the latest ad slogan, but it sounds more strategic to say it's a positioning statement.

The agency then develops a fresh ad campaign with revised media and promotions to re-position the brand and get more customers to consider buying it in its "new and improved" form. There may be additional package or store designs (bringing in some more outside experts), to demonstrate that change has happened for the better.

If it's a retailer or restaurant chain, new uniforms may also be in order. The campaign is now presented to the executive committee, and marketing anxiously waits for the charge "Let's roll with it!"

Next comes a frenzy of activity where all parties work feverishly to meet a deadline. When the pieces are almost in place, there will be a meeting with the sales or operations managers to bring them into the loop. A launch video will be produced to introduce the campaign to the field and there will be meetings and intra-net presentations to be sure that everyone understands the new campaign and the revitalized brand before it breaks to the public.

The Result of Misplaced Implementation

At that point, after the initial excitement and media hype, everyone goes back to work, and things go back to usual for both the company and the clients or customers - just as they did before the re-branding initiative. If the sales and market share problems persist, heads roll, agencies are replaced, and employees wonder why nothing seems to work. The new marketers come in with different ideas, agencies, and plans. More dollars are spent. The brand continues to be challenged.

Is this an over-simplification? Perhaps. Different situations, different products, and different organizations - things will vary depending on the circumstances. However, we maintain that this happens all too

often, because the marketing group does not take the time up front to ensure that when it's finally "time to roll," the implementation has an impact within the marketplace, and that the positioning resonates in four different, yet interrelated, ways, with the target market.

The first developmental steps of conducting research, determining the value, creating an emotional relationship, and communicating effectively and consistently, are not limited to new product introductions. These steps must be adhered to in revitalizing or repositioning a brand as well. In fact, we think it's even more critical to make sure that the changes are the right ones and the positioning is on target. As Weight Watchers tells its members, "This is not just a new diet; it's a new way of life. And you have to live it every day."

Bringing Your Brand to Life

We've talked at some length about a brand being the "DNA" of your business - the very essence of the product or service that differentiates it from all of the other choices in the marketplace. In the Implementation Phase, it's time to externalize the DNA so that it transitions from becoming a way of life *within* your organization, to *externally* becoming a part of the lives of your target clients and customers.

To begin the implementation process, you'll need to bring the DNA of your brand to life with every member of your staff. And, to ensure the success of this energizing injection of the brand's DNA into your organization, you will have to communicate the brand strategy and demonstrate it consistently - just as marketing programs are executed with your clients and customers.

To implement a brand - any brand - you have to have the right people in the right place, doing and saying the right things. In other words, you have to get your people to live up their brand every day.

Earlier, we talked about getting the entire organization involved in developing the brand, and this is critical. But even more critical is getting everyone to participate in ensuring that the brand is implemented at every touch point - on a daily basis.

By networking and involving people in the decision-making process (based on an understanding of the brand strategy), organizations can win by acclamation.

Revisiting Lexus

Lexus, as we described previously, ensures that all of its people at the dealerships are trained in the Lexus way so that everyone, from the receptionist to the people who wash your car, knows how to take care of customers and their automobiles.

Lexus had a distinct plan for how their dealers would market their brand differently from any other car company in America. They made sure their dealers (most of whom had been dealers of other American brands) understood that Lexus was unique, and that they and their entire staff had to do things totally differently from the norm.

The plan called for a unique level of experience that went far beyond consumer expectations - from the time a customer walked into the showroom to look at a new car, through the entire purchase transaction, including service, parts, and follow-up communications. They wanted a "Wow" reaction, and they created a response in

their customers that they have consistently executed for more than two decades.

While the Lexus brand has become a standard of excellence within the automotive industry, other automobile brands were not as successful because their plans were not as well executed.

Cadillac - "Break Through"

Cadillac is an excellent example. Once the luxury standard for the U.S. auto industry, Cadillac had seen its market share dwindle and its brand lose loyalty on almost every front. Seeing what Lexus was becoming, Cadillac decided to take them on with a new line of comparable automobiles under the Catera brand.

Built on the successful German Opel platform, the cars actually competed favorably with Lexus. However, that's where the similarity ended, and why that brand was a huge failure.

First, the brand was sold in a traditional Cadillac dealership, where the same inferior brand implementation carried over to the new Catera. The service had not improved and the marketing was similar to what they had used before. In other words, their DNA had not really changed, and car buyers weren't fooled! After a few lackluster years, the model was discontinued. And it was due, in great part, to inconsistent implementation at the store and customer level.

Nordstrom - "Reinvent Yourself"

Successful brands distinguish themselves by living up to their name every day. For example, sales people at Nordstrom department

store are legendary for their consistent "exceptional customer service" that goes way beyond "How can I help you?"

Nordstrom opened its doors in Seattle in 1901 and, by 1975, had become a retail giant with $100 million in sales. In a retail category suffering from changing customer preferences and expectations, this department store understood that it's the *store experience* that makes the brand special, and it has millions of loyal customers to prove it! Nordstrom's philosophy has remained unchanged for more than 100 years: offer the customer the best possible service, selection, quality, and value.

So brand implementation goes high, wide, and deep. It starts at the top, goes all the way through an organization and it doesn't ever stop. Everyone is responsible for brand success, and that's how it should be.

Market the Way They Think

In the years that we've been working with branding and the brain's buying styles, many people have asked why BrainBranding is better than other branding methods. Here's the reason: while people may look alike, their brains don't *think* alike. And most branding strategies tend to be developed based on the thinking/buying style of the person creating it, without taking other styles into account.

As you know from reading this book, the brain's different ways of processing and making purchasing decisions generates diversity - whether people are solving a problem, selecting a brand, or just reading a book. There's no way for you to know in advance how people think; using BrainBranding to manage this diversity will put you head and shoulders above your competition as you implement your brand.

> *There's no way for you to know in advance how people think; using BrainBranding to manage this diversity will put you head and shoulders above your competition as you implement your brand.*

Research says...

Earlier we spoke about the research of industrial psychologist, Carl Rogers. Because of the brain's natural thinking process, preferred words enter into your brain, and non-preferred words may be filtered out. Whatever gets triggered gets attention.

Think of them as Keywords: if your words don't match what someone's brain is poised to hear or read, then their brain tunes them out. And since you don't know which words are on the preferred list, it's a guessing game. Or perhaps not.

The BrainBranding process provides the solution: by using preferred words and symbols from *each* of the four Buying Styles, your brand gets a voice. When you develop your personal or company brand, or create your brand's marketing materials, you tend to consider *words and symbols that appeal to you* in a brand - which is completely logical. But you may be missing out on opportunities to reach a broader base of clients and customers.

Oprah - The Universal Brand

When you develop a brain-based brand that has universal appeal, what you stand for - personally and professionally - will naturally resonate with more people; in addition, it will have greater staying power and be memorable.

Let's look at the example of the Oprah Brand. Her name alone is a brand that's recognized throughout the world, and it's a great example of a positive brand with universal appeal.

- **Investigators** appreciate the factual basis of her topics and the research that goes into her website. When Denis Leary, the star of the TV series *Rescue Me*, was a guest on her show to promote his book, he said he had been skeptical (leery?) about her - was she authentic, the real deal? So he went online to her website and typed in a variety of words and topics to see what would come up (some of which cannot be printed in this book!).

  He said that he was impressed with the quality of the research he found, the breadth of topics, the professionals to whom she turned for advice, and the positive impact that the information she provided has had on millions of people. That's quite a testimonial!

- **Coordinators** are engaged by the detail, thoroughness, and structure of her programs. Nothing is left to chance because

there's a well-thought-out plan in place every step of the way. Each of her shows is organized and has a structure - it's not the same each day, but it's there. You are told what's coming next - you experience it - and then it's recapped. And that's a fairly consistent method.

- **Relaters** are captivated by her genuine caring - for people, issues, animals, and the downtrodden. Whether she's interviewing a guest who's sitting with her on the stage, interacting with the studio audience, speaking with people via Skype or video feed, or connecting to the people watching from their homes, Oprah forms a personal relationship with each and every person.

When I've asked people why they enjoy her program, they said she made them feel as if she were speaking to them directly, one-on-one. And, in a way, she is.

- **Trendsetters** have a great deal to listen and react to: Oprah asks hypothetical questions of provocative guests, weaving innovative topics, sets, performers, and performances into every program. When her TV show returned to the air in September 2009, following the summer break, she opened with an outdoor show on Chicago's "Miracle Mile." It was just another example of her ability to put her vision into action, pulling out all the stops in her search for something new and creative.

Chicken Soup for the Soul®

Here's another example of a universal brand: the *Chicken Soup for the Soul®* books. Unless you've lived in obscurity for the last

17 years, you know about the remarkable success of this book series, compiled and marketed by Mark Victor Hanson and Jack Canfield.

Over the years, the *Chicken Soup books* have expanded to include moms, dads, and teenagers with stories of inspiration and guts, tenaciousness, and tenderness. There's a lot for a brain to love with these books, because of the variety of stories and authors. In fact, the name of the book series is probably better known than the two men who published the first book in 1993.

Who's in the Driver's Seat?

Since every brain is comprised of thinking and buying styles, it makes sense to let all of them participate in your branding and marketing efforts. Otherwise, you may be missing the boat by leaving out words and images that engage the brains of *all* people in your target market.

The BrainBranding system provides the means for you to market the way people think - by putting your brain in the driver's seat and letting it lead your branding efforts.

BrainBranding and Social Media

In considering your brand's social media presence, there are four different ways of presenting it. Just having your message available on a LinkedIn or Facebook page may not be enough to attract the attention that it deserves. What may be missing? The brain's four buying styles.

The same thought and consideration that goes into brand development and implementation applies to your online presence. The information you offer about your brand's products and services has to be presented in a way that satisfies the needs of the reader, by describing them through four points of view, and four sets of "languages." Only then can you be sure that your words will both resonate, and have staying power.

Remember - it's most natural for you to write based on your own style, but you may be omitting key words from other styles. Whether you're writing for a search engine or a social media site, keep your eye on the goal: engaging the brain of the four styles.

CHAPTER 9:

PUTTING YOUR BRAIN-BRAND TO WORK

Your brand defines what people can expect from you and your business. With this newly acquired knowledge about your brain, you have the opportunity to develop a brand with much larger reach - and staying power - than ever before.

Everyone has to "buy in" before making a decision, whether it's to agree on a concept or purchase a car. Based on your own DNA, you are naturally drawn to certain products and services because of the way they "speak" to you. You may not have been aware of why that is, but now that you are, you can rethink your brand from a new perspective.

So, where do you go from here? Whether you plan to take your company's brand to new heights in market share, or whether you are taking "Brand You" to a stronger place within your organization or your own enterprise, the principles that we've covered are applicable to any situation, and are truly workable, as promised.

To give you additional clarification about where to begin, or how all of the steps fall into place, below are two brand stories that you can use as models for your unique situation. We're using as examples a

> *Everyone has to "buy in" before making a decision, whether it's to agree on a concept or purchase a car.*

consumer product and an entrepreneur, and have outlined their BrainBranding process as a template for you during your own development process.

We hope that, by following along with these examples, you'll be able to accelerate your brand's growth and outshine the competition.

EXAMPLES OF TWO BRANDS IN THE DEVELOPMENT STAGES

SINUS 1 (a consumer product): This over-the-counter nasal spray was developed by an entrepreneur and inventor in conjunction with pharmaceutical and medical professionals. Unlike many other nasal sprays and medications on the market, Sinus 1 was formulated as an antiseptic to treat the *causes* of sinusitis, rather than treat just the symptoms, such as congestion, runny nose, sneezing, coughing, and pain.

Previous research has indicated that most sinusitis is caused by the airborne mold and bacteria that we constantly breathe. Other medications treat the subsequent symptoms and often cause rebound addiction to the chemicals, resulting in exacerbating the problems, instead of bringing relief.

The new product cleanses the sinuses and, if used regularly, can prevent the onset of sinusitis or reduce the inflammation caused by it. Because the product was not developed as a drug, Sinus 1 would have to be marketed as an over-the-counter product without FDA approval. Testing Sinus 1 with hundreds of sinus sufferers produced encouraging results and enthusiastic endorsement of its efficacy.

The challenge currently facing Sinus 1 is to develop a brand that generates demand and distribution without incurring the same costs as the nationally distributed products, while creating product awareness.

HARRY JAMESON (an entrepreneur): An experienced training professional for a major financial services company, Harry has developed and/or implemented training programs for corporate personnel, headquarters staff, and management groups for several years. While not the head of Corporate Training and Development, he is the go-to person when there is a need for a new model or in-house training initiative.

Harry's presentation style and expertise make him a valuable employee, but due to the strength of upper-level management and their career stability, there is little potential for promotions or upward mobility. In addition, Harry is not the decision maker when it comes to setting strategy and corporate-wide training policy, although he believes that he is more than qualified to do so.

Harry is loyal to the company and likes the location for his family; however, he's eager to gain more responsibility and income, and feels frustrated by the time it will take him to move up the corporate ladder. He believes he is perceived as a training expert and not the leader that he is striving to become.

Working with many training organizations, he realizes there is great potential for experienced trainers like himself and an opportunity to launch his own business. Harry believes he can develop training programs, train other trainers, and also speak professionally on topics such as customer service and organizational development and change. The key, he feels, is how to differentiate himself from

the other corporate trainers and presenters in the business marketplace.

On the following pages, you will see the brand and marketing strategies we developed for these two different entities. We began by asking questions related to each of the four steps of the BrainBranding process, and then summarized the key points.

SINUS I

STEP ONE: CREATE YOUR VISION

1. Where will Sinus I market its products?
2. Will this be a mass-market product?
3. How will this product be revolutionary?
4. Will it be endorsed by major medical publications?
5. Will it be featured on national media, e.g., Dr. Oz, Today, GMA?
6. What are other line extensions that can build on the SINUS I brand?

Key Points: Sinus I is an innovative sinus product that prevents infection, rather than simply treating sinus symptoms. The nature of its preventative power demands a creative brand and marketing approach - one that is endorsed by the medical community - on major media, and in research described in publications such as *The American Journal of Medicine*.

HARRY JAMESON

STEP ONE: CREATE YOUR VISION

1. What is the best market for Harry - Corporate, Training Organizations, or Entrepreneurship?
2. Who is his typical client?
3. Will there be a staff of other trainers?
4. Will it be a national or regional venture?
5. Will Harry be a trainer, a keynoter, or both?
6. Are there specific topics that will be his trademark?
7. Should he write a book? Workbooks? Videos?

Key Points: Harry's vision is to set himself in business as a training, development, and education entrepreneur, with a focus on sales, customer service, and training trainers. He imagines a local, then regional company where he and staff would travel to other parts of the country to work with clients. Professional speaking and writing are part of his vision.

STEP TWO: CONDUCT RESEARCH 🔍	STEP TWO: CONDUCT RESEARCH 🔍
1. How many people suffer from sinusitis?	1. How much training is outsourced to the experts?
2. Who/what is the competition?	2. Is the trend toward web-based or in-house training?
3. What types of sinus problems are caused by the germs/bacteria that Sinus 1 eliminates?	3. What are the current hot topics in training?
4. What are the side effects of existing treatments?	4. How do companies select training services?
5. How pleased are people with current sinus sprays?	5. Why do companies choose their training programs?
6. How much interest is there in a new way of treating sinusitis?	6. What are the most common topics in training staff members in the professional speakers industry?
Key Points: Recent research from Harvard University indicates that of the more than 50 million people in the U.S. who suffer from chronic bouts of sinusitis, 50% have rebound effects from using decongestant sprays. Further, 75% of sinusitis sufferers require a better, stronger treatment for their symptoms.	**Key Points:** Harry's research revealed a need to combine both in-house training with online offerings. He sees the greatest potential in sales training, particularly in the financial services and health care industries. He knows from doing his research that most companies select training that will contribute to the bottom line.

STEP THREE: COMMUNICATE EMOTIONAL VALUE

1. What are the benefits of using Sinus I versus the existing products on the market?
2. How does eliminating the symptoms of sinusitis affect the lifestyle of the consumers?
3. How important is a natural (vs. chemical) treatment?
4. What are the side effects of using other products?
5. Can a sufferer avoid surgery or major medical expenses using Sinus I?
6. What are the success stories of those who have tried Sinus I and have helped their sinus attacks?
7. What are the overriding benefits a consumer will realize through using Sinus I?

Key Points: If their sinus problems are alleviated, most patients feel their lifestyle will be significantly improved, and their relationships with family, friends, and co-workers will be enhanced. They also believe that they will be more productive, because their sinus problems have been "wearing them down." They want a healthy solution without drugs or medical treatments.

STEP THREE: COMMUNICATE EMOTIONAL VALUE

1. How important is personal service to the managers who hire outside training experts?
2. How have previous audiences/classes responded to the training that Jameson has provided in the past?
3. What are the key benefits from using Jameson's training?
4. How do the relationships developed during Jameson's training continue after the program is finished?
5. What is the benefit of in-house training staffs when so much is done online?
6. How will the outcomes he obtains create long-term relationships with his clients?

Key Points: Harry's natural ability to connect to people in his workshops will serve him well as he builds his business. In addition, he has well-established relationships with training vendors that could lead to increased business. His ability to be flexible in choosing clients and venues will be a significant advantage over his competitors.

STEP FOUR: CONSTRUCT A PLAN

1. How will Sinus I be distributed?
2. How will it build awareness - Retail? Online? Both?
3. Who is the target market - doctors or consumers?
4. What are the best media options for building awareness and credibility?
5. How do you develop and market PR events to showcase the benefits of the product?
6. Endorsements - consumers or celebrities?
7. What product extensions are available now?
8. What follow-up research is necessary to provide the results needed to make the claims credible?

Key Points: The solution: build awareness about Sinus 1, and demonstrate that it is the only product that treats *the cause* of sinusitis - not just the symptoms. Since store distribution won't generate sufficient sales, they need to present testimonials from recovering patients in a factual, non-commercial format to build credibility. Promotional events must generate news coverage and feature stories to the medical community and the consumer to differentiate this product from the competition.

STEP FOUR: CONSTRUCT A PLAN

1. What training programs need to be developed?
2. What presentations can be delivered now to gain awareness and leads?
3. How can he reach the decision makers to build awareness for programs and get a personal interview/meeting?
4. What affiliations are needed to develop a network within the industry?
5. What materials (i.e., a book, workshops) need to be developed and produced?
6. What online resources in his field are needed to become a factor with search engines? With social media?

Key Points: Harry has opted for a two-pronged approach: one for online services and products and one that represents more traditional in-house training. His networking efforts, as well as his marketing materials, will reflect this strategy. In addition, Harry plans to use SEO and social media to promote his business, products, and services. Harry has a well-developed network that will provide resources, guidance, and leads as he moves forward with his plan.

These two examples should help you to create your brand by (1) asking the necessary questions to develop a brand that appeals to all four Buying Styles, (2) using words and symbols that resonate with more of your target buyers, and (3) providing the answers to shape a business implementation plan.

Please note that each one of the questions included will lead to other questions that must be answered to define your brand's DNA, and to achieve the differentiation necessary for your success. However, the template works because it follows individual natural thinking patterns, and it expands your brand's appeal to more people by determining the key elements for success.

You have seen that many brands with viable positioning have the potential to fail and go into a wasteland of "me-too" or "who cares?" By following the principles in this book and the steps that are outlined, your brand will become important, and will prosper in a truly memorable way.

CHAPTER 10:
THE END AND THE BEGINNING

We began this book with the observation - and realization - that a narrowly defined brand has less potential to be as successful compared to one that is developed with the four buying styles in mind. We examined the brand called "Joyce" and projected that, had the marketers been more mindful of understanding that Joyce - and others in her general demographic - do not all think and buy alike, that their results would have been different - and probably much better.

What we know as a result of our research is that there are diverse Joyces, each of whom has a different way of thinking, and a different buying style. Since everyone is a combination of the four thinking and buying styles, and since no two people think exactly alike, they also don't make purchases in the same way. Therefore appealing to the four styles makes a lot of sense.

When we formed our partnership, it was with the express purpose of providing a system for brand development that would (1) make your brand unique in the eyes of the consumer, (2) give your brand universal appeal in the wallets of the consumer, and (3) provide

a way for your brand to have staying power in the brains of the consumer.

Throughout the book, we've given examples of many solid brands with viable positioning that *still* have the potential to fail and go into a wasteland of "me-too" or "who cares?"

By following the BrainBranding principles, you will have the tools necessary to determine the DNA of your brand and, importantly, its core value. It's this value that you will then communicate as your message: through marketing, advertising, and social media.

BrainBranding is appropriate for many types of people, whether you're self-employed or employed by others, whether you're in a long-standing career or embarking on a new adventure, whether your business is a start-up or start over. The brand you develop is the personal symbol of who you are, what you represent, and what people can expect by doing business with you.

As a result of using the 4-step BrainBranding process, your brand will become an important fixture in the minds of consumers, and has the potential to sustain and prosper in a truly memorable way. This is a powerful remedy for the challenges of branding.

BrainBranding - what a solution!

BIBLIOGRAPHY

Boostrom, Robert. *Developing Creative and Critical Thinking*. Illinois: NTC Publishing Group, 1993.

Bueno, Bolivar J. and Matthew W Ragas. *The Power of Cult Branding*. California: Prima Publishing, 2002.

Eiffert, Stephen D. *Cross-Train Your Brain: A Mental Fitness Program for Maximizing Creativity and Achieving Success*. New York: AMA-COM Publications, 1999.

Heath, Chip and Dan Heath. *Made to Stick: Why Some Ideas Survive and Others Die*. New York: Random House, 2007.

Kim, W. Chan and Renee Mauborgne. *Blue Ocean Strategy*. Massachusetts: Harvard Business School Publishing, 2005.

Pink, Daniel H. *A Whole New Mind: Why Right-Brainers Will Rule the Future*. New York: The Berkeley Publishing Group, 2005.

Rogers, Carl. *Client-Centered Therapy: Its Current Practice, Implications and Theory*. London: Constable and Robinson, 2003.

Siler, Todd H. *Think Like a Genius*. New York: Bantam Books, 1996.

Sun Tzu and Ralph D. Sawyer. The *Art of War*. Colorado: Westview Press, 1994.

ABOUT KEN BANKS

With more than 30 years' experience in retail marketing and branding, Ken Banks established KAB Marketing to focus on helping retailers, media organizations, and advertisers to develop brand strategies and programs that better position them with today's customers. A professional speaker, Ken is in demand for presentations on branding, marketing, and advertising topics at major national meetings and conferences.

Ken has used his expertise with prominent organizations such as Procter & Gamble, Circuit City Stores, Eckerd Drugs, Dayton Hudson, Doner Advertising, Fahlgren Benito, Florida Tourism, McDonald's, and PetSmart.

In 2007 Ken and Robyn Winters co-founded BrainBranding™LLC, a company that combines the art of effective branding with the

brain's four Buying Styles, resulting in brands and brand strategies that resonate with more clients, and that have universal appeal.

Ken graduated from Wayne State University in Detroit with a B.S in Marketing. He earned his master's degree from the American Graduate School for International Management (Thunderbird) in Phoenix. Ken is currently an Adjunct Professor of Marketing at Schiller International University's Largo, Florida, campus.

Ken's passion and excellence have been recognized in his industry: Advertising Age Awards for top TV retail commercials, a Clio finalist twice, Retail Advertising Conference awards for both radio and TV, National Association of Drug Stores awards, the AAF Silver Medal, the Lifetime Achievement Award from the National Speakers Association-Central Florida, the Television Bureau's first national award for innovation in Retail Television Advertising, and induction into the Retail Advertising Hall of Fame.

Ken is a contributing author to the book *Marketing Magic,* and writes a monthly blog called "What's Branding Got to Do With It?" With Robyn Winters, Ken co-authored the articles, "How to Create a Successful Brand Strategy" in the January/February 2010 issue of *Speaker*, the official magazine of the National Speakers Association, and "Using Their Heads" in the July 2011 issue of Stores[a] magazine.

Visit Ken at www.brainbranding4.com and www.KenBanks.com.

ABOUT ROBYN WINTERS

Robyn is a business consultant, coach, and international speaker with a focus on enhancing communication and presentation effectiveness. Robyn blends the art of communication with the science of thinking and buying styles to create customized programs and presentations that engage the brain of all listeners.

Through her business, Stand Up, Stand Out!ᵃ International, Inc., Robyn works with clients who want to present themselves more successfully, and to bridge communication gaps between managers and employees, hiring professionals and job candidates, and sales people and buyers. Robyn also coaches business partners and couples to use their collective brains more advantageously and more compatibly.

Robyn has worked with a distinguished client base that includes Home Shopping Network, Delta Air Lines, American Express,

Hoffman LaRoche, American Society of Association Executives (ASAE), Hewlett Packard, McKesson, and KPMG.

As a professional speaker, she has presented at national conferences and conventions that include the National Speakers Association Annual Convention, Meeting Professionals International Southwest Conference, the Independent Community Bankers Association, and the Association of Physician Assistants in Oncology. She has been featured in *Savvy Executive Magazine of Tampa Bay*. With Ken Banks, Robyn co-authored the articles, "How to Create a Successful Brand Strategy" in the January/February 2010 issue of *Speaker*, the official magazine of the National Speakers Association, and "Using Their Heads" in the July 2011 issue of Stores[a] magazine.

Robyn holds an M.A. from Wesleyan University and is an adjunct instructor at Cornell University's Management Development Division at the School of Industrial and Labor Relations in New York City. She is certified in an array of assessment tools that include: The Myers-Briggs Type Indicator (MBTI); Tracom's Social Style Model™; and DBM's I-Speak Your Language®.

Robyn is a long-standing member of the National Speakers Association (NSA) and Business and Professional Women. She was twice The recipient of the Rosita Perez Spirit Award, given by the NSA-Central Florida chapter.

Visit Robyn at www.brainbranding4.com and www.standupstandoutinc.com.

www.ingramcontent.com/pod-product-compliance
Lightning Source LLC
Chambersburg PA
CBHW072134280526
45788CB00002B/629